Shipwrecks,
Smugglers, *and*
Maritime Mysteries

Eugene D. Wheeler

&

Robert E. Kallman

Pathfinder Publishing
Ventura, California

Shipwrecks,
Smugglers *and*
Maritime Mysteries

Published by
Pathfinder Publishing
458 Dorothy Avenue
Ventura, California 93003
(805) 642-9278

First Printing 1984
Second Edition 1986 Revised
Third Edition 1989 Revised
Fourth Printing 1996

Printed in the United States of America

Library of Congress Cataloging in Publication Data

Wheeler, Eugene D.
Shipwrecks, smugglers & maritime mysteries of the Santa Barbara Channel.
   I. Shipwrecks – California – Santa Barbara Channel.
   I. Kallman, Robert E. II. Title.
   III. Title: Shipwrecks, smugglers, and maritime mysteries of the Santa Barbara Channel.
   G525.W43 1984   979.4'91   84-25106
   ISBN 0-934793-03-4

TABLE OF CONTENTS

ACKNOWLEDGMENTS

The authors are indebted to many people and organizations for their help in writing Shipwrecks, Smugglers, and Maritime Mysteries. For valuable data and stories of harbor accidents and shipwrecks, we thank the staffs of the Channel Islands, Port Hueneme and Ventura harbors. Assistance was also provided by the staff of the Channel Islands National Park Service and John B. Richards of the University of California Sea Grant Program, Cooperative Extension - Marine Advisory Program. The Coast Guard contributed by giving us information about accidents in their jurisdiction. The librarians of the Santa Barbara News-Press, Ventura Star-Free Press, the Ventura County Historical Society Museum and the Santa Barbara Historical Society cheerfully provided us with space to work, their shipwreck files and useful suggestions. Fine photographs were made available to us by A. L. Lundy, Pandora Snethkamp, Bob Wake, the Star Free-Press, the Santa Barbara and Ventura Historical Society Museums.

We appreciate the assistance given by Don Knight, Archie Bard, Gerald Barney, Grant Heil, Walter Hoffman, Karen Jensen, Karen Lyders, Faith O'Leary, Richard Whitehead and others for reviewing our manuscript and book concepts, and also for sharing their knowledge of the Channel, boating accidents and wrecks.

Appreciation is offered to Eugenie Wheeler and Kathy Stinson for reviewing and editing the manuscript. Many others assisted by providing us with articles, interviews and their comments during the preparation of the book. We thank all of you.

Eugene D. Wheeler & Robert E. Kallman

DEDICATION

This book is dedicated to those rescuers who have risked their lives so that others might survive.

INTRODUCTION

Those new to the Santa Barbara Channel may wonder why the U.S. Coast Guard cutter at Santa Barbara is one of the busiest in the Guard's entire fleet. After sailing through a season or two in the Channel, they understand.

All kinds of vessels, new and old, have been battered, run aground and sunk during the fury of the surprisingly sudden storms in the Channel. Experienced professional and recreational sailors learn to appreciate the fickelness of its weather. But even the professionals, with their accumulated knowledge, have made mistakes and paid for them with personal injuries or their lives.

The Channel has a rich history. A race has vanished from its shores. Different cultures have been engulfed by immigrants. The Channel has many mysteries. Ships, planes, and people have disappeared without a trace or an explanation. Smugglers, pirates, and outlaws have ranged its waters--and continue to do so. The same coves are used for smuggling today that were used during prohibition in earlier times. Piracy and murder still occur.

Many accidents and shipwrecks are unknown because no record keeping authority existed in the early history of the Channel. Because no central authority exists even today to collect information on all accidents, many are not reported. The marine accident information in this book comes from many different sources; books on shipwrecks, special studies, environmental impact reports, newspapers, harbor districts, Coast Guard, Navy, state agencies, county authorities and old salts. The authors have gleaned information from all known sources, but have included the most interesting and unusual stories.

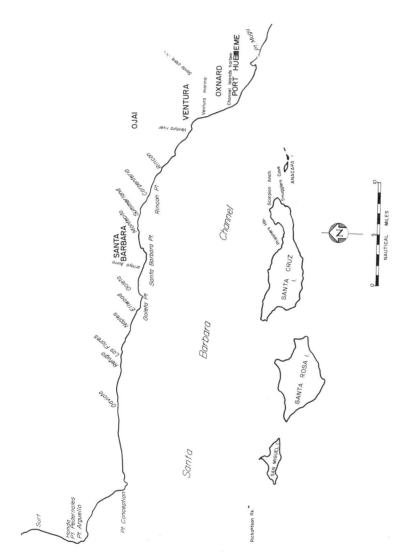

Locational map of cities and points of interest in text.

ONE

EARLY CHANNEL EXPLORERS
AND ACCIDENTS

Flying high over the Santa Barbara Channel, it is difficult to believe that the placid-looking sea glistening in the sunlight below has been so volatile and violent over the centuries. Wedged between its four Islands and the mainland, the Channel deceives fishermen, boaters, divers, swimmers and fliers by its tranquil look. Inexperienced sailors often start for the Channel Islands from the mainland in the morning thinking the seas will remain calm. Many discover too late that the Channel can become dangerously turbulent.

The Channel's rocky shoreline is unforgiving to sailors who make a navigational error or are driven off course by its unusual weather. No ship or aircraft is exempt from the Channel's wrath regardless of size or extent of electronic equipment on board. The "Devils Jaw," as Point Conception is sometimes called, and other forbidding shorelines of the Channel, are littered with the memories of terrifying wrecks of small and large vessels. Many a ship has rammed into one of the Islands, believing until too late that the shore was miles away.

From a dead calm, winds can sweep up to 50 knots or more in seconds. Winds can change direction radically with startling suddeness. Monstrous waves can evolve in minutes from a flat sea. Fog can appear as if by magic complete with invisible ships sounding their eerie horns. Currents can change direction and force without warning. Sailors are confronted with strange weather, even tidal waves. The largest tidal wave to swamp a California shore struck the Santa Barbara coast. It was caused by one of the greatest earthquakes in California's history which had had its epicenter in the Channel.

The Earliest Navigators of the Channel

The earliest known Channel sailors, the Chumash Indians, learned that the weather and sea could be devastating. About 1,000 years ago, the Santa Barbara Channel Indians started building seagoing plank canoes that they used for fishing and trading trips to the Channel Islands. The canoes were 25 to 26 feet long and were rowed by two to four men using double-ended paddles. The canoes had a beam of three and one half feet, weighed about 350 pounds, and could carry several people or a cargo of around 4,000 pounds.

Because of the Channel's winds and weather and numerous sinkings, the Indians timed their crossings carefully. When traveling to the Islands from the mainland, the Indians avoided trips directly across the Channel. They followed a route that hugged the mainland coast until they reached what is now Port Hueneme, the mainland point closest to the Islands. They then paddled to Anacapa Island, a distance of twelve miles, and reached the other islands by traveling west.

First European Explorers Encounter the Channel

Juan Rodriguez Cabrillo was the first known European explorer to visit the Channel. Cabrillo, a Portuguese navigator in the Spanish service, was sent northward on an exploring journey

Chumash Indian Canoe

with two caravelles, the *San Salvador*, acting as Flag-ship and her consor, the *Vitoria*. They arrived in the Channel on October 10, 1542 and anchored near the Chumash town of Xuco, near the original town of San Buenaventura. On the 14th, they anchored just off the present location of Santa Barbara. They found the Indians to be very friendly and brought them fish and other foods in their canoes to barter. The expedition's navigator, Bartolome Ferrel, who recorded Cabrillo's explorations, reported that the Spanish were amazed at the large number of Indians living on the Islands and along the coast.

During most of October and the first half of November, they spent time travelling around the Channel and the Islands naming them La Posesion (San Miguel), San Lucas (Santa Rosa), San Salvador (Santa Cruz) and possibly Vitoria (Anacapa). Point Concepcion was named Cape Galera.

Before the little fleet's departure from the Channel, on November 11, 1542, Cabrillo fell and broke his arm on San Miguel Island. The on-board "doctor" wrapped a splint around the arm which he carried in a sling. Apparently, Cabrillo didn't take the broken arm too seriously, as the expedition continued northward of Point Concepcion along the California coast. Cabrillo and his small fleet encountered a severe storm near Pigeon Point, north of Monterey Bay and turned back. They retreated back to Cuyler Harbor on San Miguel Island, arriving on November 23, a journey of twelve days. Throughout the northern trip Cabrillo was in pain as his arm would not heal properly. Gangrene had set in. On January 3, 1543, Juan Rodriguez Cabrillo died.

Overlooking the harbor at San Miguel Island was a Chumash village that was built at the fork of two small streams that were present at the time. Cabrillo was buried by his men and some tribal members at this fork. Cabrillo's grave site has never been found because over the last 400 years earthquakes, tidal waves and slides have forced a nearby bluff to "sluff-off" and to cover the site with thousands of tons of earth.

Before Cabrillo died, he ordered the expedition to continue northward. Bartolome Ferrelo, a Levantine pilot mayor, assumed command. On February 18, 1543 the fleet sailed north again. By the 28th of February they reached Trinidad Head and turned back, again because of a major storm. Apparently, the expedition passed by the entrance to the San Francisco Bay, but did not venture into it. They arrived back in the Santa Barbara Channel on March 5th and anchored off Xuco again. On March 7, 1543, the fleet headed south, ending the first European exploration of "Alto California."

Nearly four centuries later the first U.S. Navy Fleet Admiral, visiting the Santa Barbara Channel for the first time with the 'Great White Fleet' died also of a strange and sudden illness.

Many explorations and adventures in the Channel have gone unheeded as many voyages were unrecorded. After discovering Chumash Indian drawings of Chinese junks in caves along the coast, some historians think the Chinese may have visited the Santa Barbara Channel before the Spanish did. As no Chinese artifacts have been found on the coast nor records from China describing such visits, it can only be surmised.

Explorer Sebastian Vizcaino

In 1602, the Spanish explorer Sebastian Vizcaino visited the Santa Barbara Channel, the Islands, and the mainland while sailing northward from New Spain, or Mexico, in search of a California port. Father Ascension, who was with Vizcaino, wrote

A Spanish Caravelle

of the voyage into the Channel: "After we left the port of San Diego (named by Vizcaino), we discovered many islands placed in a line, one behind the other. Most of them were inhabited by many friendly Indians who have trade and commerce with those of the mainland."

The Spanish made no attempts at colonization until nearly two centuries later. However, they continued to sail through the Santa Barbara Channel on a regular basis after discovering a return route eastward from the Phillipines in 1565. The Spanish ships made their landfall in Northern California and sailed south along the California Coast to Panama. Other explorers, British, Russian, and French also made voyages to the Channel.

Mystery of the Abandoned Cannon

Sir Francis Drake, on his voyage of exploration north to San Francisco in 1579, probably sailed through the Santa Barbara Channel. Five ancient cannon found in the surf in 1981 may prove he visited the Channel or indicate who some of the other early European visitors were.

On January 21, 1981, a beachwalker found two rock-encrusted objects about half a mile east of Goleta Beach Park. Returning the next day at low tide, he found three more exposed by the scouring surf. The following day, assisted by volunteers from the University of California at Santa Barbara's Archeology and History Departments and by rangers from the County Park Department, he managed to haul the five cannon out of the surf. Using rope and steel bars, they lifted the barrels, which weighed several hundred pounds each, one at a time, and walked them through the slippery rocks and boiling surf to firm sand. Under the envious eyes of professional salvagers, the artifacts were kept under guard at the beach until moved to the nearby University campus.

The cannon, muzzle loaders, about five feet long and heavily encrusted with asphaltum and rocks, were found almost in a straight line across 50 feet of beach. Several weeks after the discovery, the State Parks Department conducted an underwater magnatometer search of the area offshore from the discovery spot in an attempt to locate any shipwreck or other artifacts. Nothing more was found.

Hauling a cannon out of the surf, 1982. (UCSB photo)

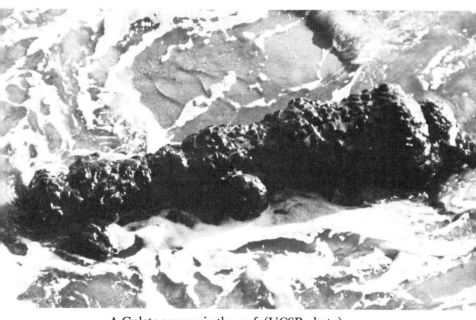

A Goleta cannon in the surf. (UCSB photo)

Since treasure hunters from all over the state descended on the area as soon as news of the discovery hit the media, the County Sheriff and Park Rangers established a tight patrol of the site. The origin of the five cannon was a source of controversy. Experts advanced at least two theories of which both had strong adherents. The most popular hypothesis was that Sir Francis Drake left them behind during repairs to the *Golden Hind* at Goleta Slough in 1579. This was based on the description in Drake's log of a "faire and good baye," and the fact that in 1891 wood cutters working in an oak grove to the west of the Slough discovered a Sixteenth Century iron anchor in the mud at the edge of the water. Identified as the type of anchor used by Cabrillo and Drake, the relic was found at a spot where vegetation indicated that a freshwater spring had flowed freely prior to the great flood of 1861. The spring was a regular stopping place for Spanish and American ships for filling their water casks. Sailing ships commonly anchored off their watering holes. The secret of why a valuable anchor was abandoned in such an easily recoverable place is a mystery that has remained unsolved for almost 100 years.

English records show that the *Golden Hind* stopped for emergency repairs at a bay in Alta California in the last years of the Sixteenth Century and that the ship entered her English port with five cannon and one anchor missing. Unfortunately, the ship's log, reportedly given to Queen Elizabeth, is not available for scrutiny.

Although supporters of the Drake theory believed that they were right, an equally strong opinion was shared by several authorities who believed that the cannon were from the English ship *Content*. A part of Thomas Cavendish's 1587 round-the-world exploration, the ship became separated from the body of the expedition somewhere off the tip of Baja California. The last recorded sighting of the *Content* was near Cabo San Lucas. The ship was never heard from or seen again.

Proponents of this theory state that the discovery in 1974 of a 1567 English silver sixpence on the shore of the North San Francisco Bay Basin is conclusive proof that Drake landed north of the Golden Gate at San Quentin Cove in Marin County in the summer of 1579. Evidence provided by U.S. Navy x-rays of two of the cannon show that they were of Sixteenth Century English design and manufacture. When Drake supporters say that there is no known record that Stephen Hare's ship, the *Content*, was ever within a thousand miles of the Santa Barbara Channel, *Content* advocates claim that the ship disappeared in the Pacific and it would be natural to assume that Hare would cling to the coast if his vessel was in need of repair. Another theory is that the cannon were a part of Spanish shore batteries that were washed off their cliff emplacements.

The secret of the cannon will not be revealed until the long and tedious task of removing the encrustations and the anticipated layer of oxidized iron beneath the tar and rocks is completed. It is hoped that as was the tradition of the time, the name of the maker or other inscriptions will be found and will identify the origin of the relics. In the meantime, the mystery and controversy of the cannon continues, as they undergo treatment years after their discovery.

The Tide Rises, The Tide Falls

Darkness settles on roofs and walls,
But the sea, the sea, in the darkness calls;
The little waves, with their soft, white hands,
Efface the footprints in the sands,
And the tide rises, the tide falls.

By Henry Wadsworth Longfellow

TWO

TRADING, SMUGGLING AND PIRACY
1800 to 1850

A few years after the Spanish began the colonization of the Santa Barbara Channel coastline in 1782, other nations learned of the sea otters, seals, and whales in the Channel. Sailing vessels came from Europe, South America, Russia, and Asia to hunt them and to trade goods.

Trading and Smuggling In The Channel

By 1810, the Spanish colonies in Mexico and South America, tired of the Spanish government's control and inefficiency, made attempts to gain greater freedom. With unrest in the North and South American colonies and more pressing matters elsewhere, Spain gave less attention to the missions in California. The missions could supply most of their food needs, but having no manufactured goods, depended on Spain and Mexico for clothing and household supplies. The California colonies came to depend on smugglers to provide illicit goods from illegal traders as Mexico lost interest in them and stopped sending supply ships to the missions. The supply situation became especially bad after 1810.

Cattle Raising and Shipping of Hides

When the Spanish colonized the shoreline area of Santa Barbara and Ventura, they brought with them cattle which rapidly multiplied. Due to the demand for hides in Europe and the eastern seaboard of the United States, an active trade soon developed with Europe and the East Coast for hides from the California Coast. Ships from New England and other countries were soon making the hazardous trip around Cape Horn to California to trade manufactured clothing and goods for hides to be taken back to Boston and other locations to be made into shoes and other leather products.

Sea Otter Trading In the Channel

In Adele Ogden's book, *The California Sea Otter Trade, 1784-1848*, she estimated that about 674 trading ships visited California from 1784 to 1836 from places like Nantucket and Boston, France, Spain, Russia, Mexico, England, Germany, Columbia, Central America, Chile, Peru, Ecuador, Hawaiian Islands and Asia. In the same period, 141 different ships made 232 port visits to Santa Barbara. The world was learning about the Channel Islands basin.

Lelia Bryd

One of the first ships of importance involved in the sea otter trade in the Channel was the *Lelia Byrd*. This 74 ton vessel out of Salem, Massachusetts, arrived on April 1, 1801, under Capt. William Shaler and a crew of nine. She completed a successful four year commercial voyage in the Pacific which made a fortune for her owner.

From 1801 to 1804 the *Lelia Byrd* sailed in and out of the Channel until she was sold to the King of the Sandwich Islands. Capt. Shaler published a report on California and the Santa Barbara Channel in 1808 which drew attention to virtues of the area. He stated, "The sea-otter of the Channel were better than on any other part of the coast. . . . American traders had left, perhaps, twenty-five thousand dollars annually on the coast in exchange for furs, in spite of the Spanish government, which was trying to discourage this type of trade."

Illegal Trading and Smuggling

American and English ships often went first to the Channel Islands where they unloaded most of their cargo and then reported to either Santa Barbara or Monterey authorities to obtain a trading permit and pay duties on less goods to be sold than they actually had. Later the hidden goods were traded with local inhabitants. In exchange for manufactured goods, the Californians traded furs and skins (sea otter, seal, beaver, bear, fox and deer), hides and tallow, fresh fruits and vegetables.

During the period when the Missions were forbidden to trade with anyone except an authorized Spanish ship, the mission padres and presidio inhabitants found means to circumvent the ruling. After initial contact with the colonists, smugglers often took their ships to Refugio, several miles west of Santa Barbara, where goods were taken ashore and traded for mission food and hides.

Spanish Take Action

By 1805 Spanish authorities strongly resented the presence of Americans and their trading and smuggling with the Californians and took various precautions. Reinforcements were made at the northern presidios and orders given that all ports were closed to foreign ships, and to make reprisals against the English. Governor Arrillaga asked the Viceroy for an armed warship to protect the coast and catch any Yankee smugglers. In March of 1805 the armed *Princesa* was sent to California.

Arrillaga targeted the Americans and ordered all commanders to intercept American smugglers, capture them and send the captives to Mexico. In 1806 four crewmen from the American ship *Peacock* were taken prisoner and sent south by the Spanish after the ship had stopped at San Miguel Island to trade and replenish provisions.

Russian fur hunting trips to the Channel were successful and became more frequent. Ships were averaging 1,050 otter-skins each. By 1806 the mission friars were their best customers. At this time the Spanish used their shore batteries to discourage foreign ships from anchoring in their ports. By 1810, more than a dozen foreign ships were operating within the Channel. The Spanish sent three vessels, the *Concepcion, San Carlos*, and the *Princesa* to patrol the coast. The Santa Barbara presidio arsenal was increased to eight cannon, which ranged from one to six pounders, and 66 soldiers, excluding various other officers in the area.

Because of the strife and revolution during the period 1811-1820 when Mexicans liberated themselves from Spain, no supplies were available from the south to the missions. As a result, trade commenced with Lima, Peru with arrival of two ships, the *Flora* and the *Tagle*.

American Smuggler Captured

The first American ship captured for smuggling by the Spanish in the Channel was the *Mercury*, under the command of George W. Ayres. While anchored a short distance above Santa Barbara on June 2, 1813, Capt. Noe on the *Flora* sailed alongside and boarded the smuggler, capturing the officers and crew and took them to the presidio. The ambitious Capt. Noe claimed the *Mercury* as a prize. He turned over $16,000 in coin from the *Mercury* to the Presidio authorities, left his own vessel at Santa Barbara and continued on planning to capture other smugglers about the Channel Islands.

In August of 1814, the *Tagle* under Jose Cavenecia sighted the American Brig *Pedler* as she entered the bight of San Luis Obispo. After the *Tagle* hoisted Spanish colors and fired a blank charge, the *Pedler* moved out toward the sea. Then the *Tagle* fired cannon balls from two guns which caused the *Pedler* to heave to. Twenty-five men from the *Tagle* boarded the *Pedler* and took possession of her. The crew was taken prisoner and the ship sailed to Santa Barbara where her hatches were locked.

Lydia Taken

In January of 1816, the Hawaiian schooner *Lydia* and the *Albatross* anchored at Refugio after a voyage from Sitka. The Santa Barbara presidio Commandante Gurrea and a handful of men boarded and arrested the two captains and took the *Lydia* to Santa Barbara. As the *Albatross* was too well armed to be taken, she sailed off after informing the Mexicans that they would return in eight days to check on the captains. The commandante released the two officers on March 15th to the *Albatross*.

PIRATES IN THE CHANNEL

George Compton First Known Pirate in Channel

One of the first known pirates to operate in the Channel was an Englishman, George Compton, in the 1750s. Compton's targets were the Galleons from Manila. Compton was born in Bristol, England. After serving on a ship to Veracruz, Mexico, he was forced by the Spaniards to flee the country. Compton traveled to Panama where he teamed up as a mariner with a band of pirates, who later chose him as their leader. They captured a Spanish Galleon lying in port at Panama with a great treasure aboard that financed their piratical adventures to the north.

Toward the end of 1753 when Compton first arrived in the Channel, his target was the *San Sebastian*, a Manila Galleon. Confronted by the pirate ship, the Spanish captain decided to run for it to the south. Compton caught up with it and sank the Spanish ship off San Clemente Island. Mission records indicate that Compton's crew were very barbarous and cruel to the survivors of the San Sebastian and other Spanish ships. He was considered the "scourge" of the California coast.

Pirate Hippolyte de Bouchard

Pirates soon became aware of the productivity of the missions and the availability of water, food supplies and furs in the Basin. One of the best known early pirates in the Santa Barbara Channel was a Frenchman Captain Hippolyte de Bouchard who commanded the Buenos Ayrean privateer, *Argentina*. This ship, armed with 38 guns and two light howitzers was also known as the *Frigata Negra*. Part of Bouchard's fleet was the *Santa Rosa*, commanded by Lt. Pedro Conde, with 26 guns and referred to as *Frigata Chica*. The two ships contained a force of 285 men from different nations.

In November of 1815, Bouchard's force attacked and looted Monterey. They destroyed and burned much of the village and presidio and knocked out all but two of the onshore guns. They stayed a week in Monterey stripping the town of munitions, clothing and anything else of value. Satisfying themselves that nothing of value remained, they burned most of the houses in town.

The pirates headed south, anchoring at Refugio Bay west of Santa Barbara on December 2, 1818. Refugio was a noted rendezvous for smugglers in Spanish days as in modern times. Ample water was available at Refugio. While Bouchard was ashore with part of his crew, Sgt. Carillo with 30 Mexican soldiers captured three of the pirates by lassoing them like cattle. The men were taken to the Presidio in Santa Barbara. Bouchard, in anger at finding most of the cattle and food supplies removed by the residents, burned and destroyed several ranch buildings. He then went to Santa Cruz Island for water and wood supplies. Bouchard returned to Santa Barbara Bay on December 6, 1818. He was in an ugly mood and wanted his men back.

The Commander of the Presidio had a tough decision. His 50-some men were outnumbered by the 285 trained and aggressive fighters on Bouchard's ships. Thinking quickly, the Presidio Commandante decided to put up a brave front. Reportedly, he marched his small band up and down the beach, but had them make changes in their clothing each time they went behind a thicket on the beach. Bouchard, watching the apparently large number of men on the beach, decided it might be wise to negotiate for the release of the three men. By accident, Bouchard's men had captured a local Mexican. The pirate offered to exchange his prisoner for the three held by the Mexican soldiers.

After much negotiation, the men were exchanged with the understanding that the pirates would leave Santa Barbara unharmed. Bouchard's fleet then hoisted anchor and sailed south. Having heard of the trouble in Santa Barbara, Ventura residents, fearing an attack, collected their valued possessions and climbed into the nearby hills for safety. Luckily for the Venturans, Bouchard sailed past them on his way southward.

San Juan Capistrano was not so lucky. On December 14, 1818, Bouchard sacked the village with a vengeance. Mexican soldiers under Jose de las Guerra were sent from Santa Barbara to reinforce the village but arrived too late. An additional 30 men had been sent from San Diego to resist Bouchard, but were ineffective. Bouchard damaged San Juan Capistrano severely in the process of looting it. Apparently well supplied now, he bypassed the frightened people in San Diego and continued on to South America.

American Piracy Fails

The crew of the schooner *Eagle,* while anchored in Santa Barbara Bay in September, 1822, boarded the American smuggling ship *Francisco de Paula,* previously named the *Cossack.* The crew claimed that they owned the ship through a previous "irregularity of sale." The *Eagle's* crew commenced to tow the *Francisco* out of the harbor. Mexican soldiers on shore fired their cannon at the *Eagle* to prevent the ship's being kidnapped. In avoiding the cannon fire to escape, the *Eagle* ran into a large kelp bed and became stuck. The Presidio soldiers captured the *Eagle*, brought the crew ashore and imprisoned them. Santa Barbara authorities sold the *Eagle* at an auction for a reported $3,000 to the Fathers of the Mission. The padres renamed it the *Santa Apolonio* and used it as a trading ship for many years.

Industrious Padre

Seeing the need for trade and ships, an industrious Santa Barbara padre, Father Luis Martinez, built a 25-ton, 2-masted ship at Avila Landing in 1812. He used the ship extensively in the buying and selling of grain and other goods in Monterey. After making a small fortune, he gave up trading, converted his profits into doubloons and planned a trip. To hide the gold from any possible pirates, he sewed the coins into a strange quilted leather tunic. He arranged passage and sailed on another ship to Lima, Peru, wearing the heavy tunic. It was such a strange, heavy garment to be wearing in hot weather that the ship's captain, Wilson, asked about it. The Father told Captain Wilson of the gold quilted into it. The Captain prevailed on the Father to lock the coat in his cabin for the duration and enjoy the voyage.

Prisoners Escape From Santa Cruz Island

In 1830, the government of Mexico decided more colonists were needed in the Santa Barbara Channel Basin to more firmly establish their dominance over the area. Recruiting inmates from prisons, authorities loaded volunteer prisoners aboard a coastal ship and sent them to Santa Barbara. The Barbarenos reacted with indignation and fear as they watched the desperadoes stream off the vessel. A meeting of townspeople and mission padres resulted in gathering the gang of cutthroats together, where the citizens convinced the newcomers that their future was linked to developing a cattle ranch on deserted Santa Cruz Island. A collection was held and enough money raised to supply cattle and provisions along with a one-way ticket for the convicts to homestead the Island.

Landing them in a cove that later become know as Prisoners' Harbor, the Mexican immigrants were left to fend for themselves. The convicts became convinced that the program wouldn't work. Slaughtering their steers, they reportedly lashed the green hides around pine logs and formed rafts. The innovative convicts shoved off from Prisoners' for the mainland. It is reported that sharks, attracted by the blood on the hides, attacked them and many were killed. Another story, probably more credible, says that they made it to Carpinteria and were assimilated into the community.

CHANNEL STORMS AND FORCES

Pilgrim Confronts Channel Storms

After a voyage of 150 days from Boston, Richard Henry Dana, on board the *Pilgrim*, arrived in Santa Barbara January 14, 1835. The first landfall was Point Conception. The *Pilgrim* sailed south to Santa Barbara, where it was anchored about three miles offshore. The Captain's fear of the Channel's notorious southeast winds, which could blow them ashore, accounted for his anchoring so far offshore. The *Pilgrim* had come to buy hides for the eastern market.

Only one other ship was in the harbor at the time—an English brig of about 300 tons. The *Pilgrim* was 86 feet long and weighed 180 tons. Dana described the Santa Barbara area as being "a low plain with mountains in the background, but the level area near the sea was entirely without trees." The Presidio and the surrounding Santa Barbara community was about half a mile inland from the beach. The Mission and support buildings were about a mile from the beach. While Dana was in Santa Barbara, two other ships came in, one from Genoa, Italy, and the other from Oahu, Hawaii, then called the "Sandwich Islands."

A Southeaster Hits

One night the Captain's fears were justified when a southeast wind came up at midnight. All ships in the harbor quickly raised sails, left their anchors attached to buoys and sailed into mid-channel with sails doublereefed before the fierce winds. Dana wrote in *Two Years Before the Mast* that the *Pilgrim* "beat about for five days in the offing, under close sail with continual rain and high seas and winds." The southeast winds were referred to as "the bane of the coast of California."

The *Pilgrim* Experiences a Point Conception Storm

Later that same January on the way north to Monterey for a trading permit, the *Pilgrim* sailed near Point Conception under full sail. By 1835, Point Conception was already known as a very windy and dangerous place. In Dana's words: "Any vessel does well which gets by it without a gale, especially in the winter season." Under heavy sail, the *Pilgrim* encountered such fierce winds at Point Conception that it heeled over greatly, frightening not only the passengers but the crew as well. Suddenly, sails and equipment seemed to let go everywhere aloft. Sails were flying everywhere. Orders were flying from the Captain, "'Haul down,' 'crew up,' 'royals, flying jib and studding sails,' all at once." Sails were flapping loose all over the boat. Several yardarms had broken and were swinging about dangerously. Dana was aloft to take in the main top gallant studding sail when he was ordered by the Captain to furl the main royal. On the shuddering, weaving ship, he had to work his way up and down masts and onto yards to pull in the sails. He described the frightening experience:

> . . . I went up on the yard; there was a worse mess, if possible, than I had left below. The braces had been let go and the yard was swinging about like a turnpike gate and the whole sail having blown out to leeward, the lee leach was over the yardarm, and the skysail was all adrift and flying about my head....I took a look below. Everything was in confusion on deck. The little vessel was tearing through the water as if she had lost her wits, the seas flying over her, and the mast leaning over at a wide angle from the vertical. At the other royal masthead was Stimson, working away at the sail, which was blowing from him as fast as he could gather it in. The top gallant sail below me was soon clued up which relieved the mast, and in a short time I got my sail furled and went below.[1]

Dana went on to say: "Before night it began to rain; and we had five days of rainy, stormy weather, under close sail all the time and were blown several hundred miles off the coast."[2]

It took the *Pilgrim* over two weeks to reach Monterey, a distance of about 100 miles, because they were beating into a headwind. When they returned to Santa Barbara a few weeks later from Monterey, it took them only 30 hours to their anchorage.

Powerful Channel Forces Ruled Havoc

Basin sailors and dwellers learned early that forces existed of unbelievable power that struck with disastrous impact when on a rampage. On December 21, 1812, an earthquake estimated at X on the Rossi-Rorel Scale (8.3 Richter magnitude) struck Southern California. It was the most severe earthquake ever recorded in Santa Barbara and was followed by aftershocks for four and a half months.

The December shakes were preceded by a series of shocks starting in May of that year. Although 1812 was most certainly the year for earthquakes in the Santa Barbara Channel, the December shock was the one best remembered because of its severity.

The epicenter was probably a submarine fault offshore from Santa Barbara and Lompoc; the intensity of the quake equalled the infamous 1906 San Francisco earthquake. Five gigantic seismic tsunamis roared on shore, tumbling buildings like matchsticks all the way inland to the front of the Santa Barbara Presidio itself. A Franciscan father in his journal described the waves as "like a high mountain of water," probably 50 feet in height. The islands also suffered. At the Canada Lobo Canyon on Santa Rosa Island an enormous earth-surface crack opened up that was 1,000 yards long, over 100 feet wide, and 50-60 feet deep. Huge boulders and rocks tumbled and rolled down the cliffs. The Indians were so frightened that they asked the Spanish to evacuate them to the mainland.[3]

The 1812 earthquake in the Channel generated the largest tsunamis ever recorded in California. The water receded out to sea about 1,500 feet on Santa Rosa Island and the other islands, exposing the ocean bottom with its rocks, shoals, and kelp beds. It happened so quickly that countless fish were stranded and flapped about high and dry. The waves were spaced about 15 minutes apart, but it was the third or fourth crest that produced the most destruction. The frightened Indians expected to be engulfed by the returning sea.

The largest wave, reported as being 50 feet high, formed off Goleta. The United States Geological Survey estimated that the wave height was actually 48-50 feet above sea level. The peak of the 1812 tsuami occurred just west of Santa Barbara. As the sea swept inland, the people along the coast ran to high ground and to the Santa Barbara and Ventura missions to escape the incoming waves. The huge waves and the earth's continual shaking for 23 days kept the Indian and Spanish population in constant fear.[4]

A temporary church was built on higher ground above the Ventura Mission. The reason for the Church's evacuation was explained by Padre Senan on January 9, 1813: "the ocean waves were considerable, although they did not occur with such force and frequency as from December to February."[5]

A large American ship in the act of smuggling contraband in Refugio Cove allegedly was carried by waves over half a mile up Refugio Canyon to a spot below former President Ronald Reagan's ranch and was then returned to the sea by the receding water, apparently unharmed.

The Chumash Indians, too, fled before the waves to higher ground. Some Indians living on the Channel Islands took to the sea in fear that the trembling Islands would disappear into the Pacific Ocean.

The few buildings in the pueblo were in ruins after the initial quake, and the Mission was almost demolished. Most of the roofs of the Presidio of Santa Barbara were on the ground in piles of rubble. Mission Purisima Concepceon, about 10 miles northeast of Point Arguello, was also destroyed.

As the aftershocks continued day after day, landslides of huge magnitude occurred on the slopes of the coastal range, further terrifying the natives. As if to portend the end of the earth, numbers of small 'volcanoes,' belching forth a mixture of water and mud, smelling like rotten eggs, appeared in many places near the Mesa area of Santa Barbara.

Several asphalt springs flowed along the coast. A burning oil or gas spring near Rincon Point erupted like a small Mount Vesuvius and continued to burn for more than a hundred years

21

after the quake. An oil spout was observed at the shoreline near what was later to become the location of the Summerland oil fields.

The Seismological Society of America estimated that from 1769 to 1928, 81 earthquakes occurred in the Santa Barbara Channel, varying in intensity from I to the maximum of X, based on the Rossi-Forel Scale. An 'X' was considered to be a great disaster, where fissures appeared in the earth's surface and mountain slides occurred.

Great Santa Barbara 'Simoon'

Santa Barbara is noted for having one of the most pleasant climates in the world. On occasions it has not been so. The drought of 1856-57 was particularly bad and a prelude to coming disaster. Probably the greatest temperature change in one day in North America occurred in the Santa Barbara/Ventura area on June 17, 1859. In June, the temperature normally ranges in the 70s and low 80s along the coast. Around noon on June 17, the temperature was an unusually warm 100 degrees for the clear sunny day. Early in the afternoon, a hot air current swept into the Channel Basin from the north. It was similar to what is known as a 'simoon' in the Arabian desert, a hot, poisonous wind. Old-timers immediately recognized that this was not the usual Santana that regularly hits the area with hot winds from the deserts to the east.

The searing blast drove residents to their homes or churches as the furnace-like heat almost wiped out the animal and bird population. Cattle dropped dead, even under the shelter of oak trees. The temperature quickly rose to an unbelievable 133 degrees. For three hours, the temperature held steadily at 130 degrees. Around five in the afternoon, the weather cooled to 122 degrees. A U.S. Coast Survey engineering boat was in the Channel that day and officially recorded the temperature at 133 degrees Fahrenheit at 2:00 p.m.

The sun was obscured by dense clouds of dust. A Coast Survey report published ten years later in 1869 said: "No human being could withstand such heat out of doors." Fortunately, the thick adobe walls of most buildings protected the inhabitants from the death-dealing winds. Fruit dropped off trees and withered on the ground. All vegetation was scorched and crops were ruined for the year.

At 5:00 p.m. the simoon winds died off and the temperature dropped to 122 degrees. As the population cautiously left the shelter of their adobe homes, they discovered that their beautiful coastal plain resembled a fire-swept desert. Animals and plants were devastated. Birds and animals lay dead as far as the eye could see. Many larger animals, exhausted, seemed on the verge of dying from the heat.

The hot desert blast withdrew as rapidly as it had come to the Channel. By seven in the evening, the temperature had dropped to 77 degrees to the great relief of every living thing that remained.

Santa Barbara amazingly held the record for the highest temperature recorded in North America until 1935 when the temperature reached 134 degrees in Death Valley, the logical place to hold the record. The record temperature in Santa Barbara was a prelude to a disastrous drought.

SAILING SHIP VICTIMS--1754 to 1849

From 1754 to 1849 seven known ships were sunk in the Channel area; three ships near Santa Barbara-Goleta, two at Point Conception, one at San Miguel, and one at San Nicholas Island. The unknown vessel that sank off the northwest tip of San Miguel Island in nearly 90 feet of water, reportedly went down in 1801. A Chinese or Japanese junk sank in March of 1815 and lies in 50 feet of water near Point Conception, the first of many to meet their fate near the treacherous point. An active Pacific Coast trading ship, the *John Begg*, rammed onto Begg Rock (named after the ship) on San Nicholas Island in 1846. The schooner *Fama* (later the *San Buenaventura*) ran aground and was stranded at Daniels Hill, Goleta, in February of 1846 near the location where the first known sailing ship was reportedly constructed in southern California in 1829. A brig, the *Francisco*, was driven ashore in a storm near Santa Barbara with a cargo of hides in November of 1847.

Rocked in the Cradle of the Deep

And such the trust that still were mine,
Though stormy winds swept o'er the brine,
Or though the tempests fiery breath
Roused me from sleep to wreck and death,
In ocean cave, still safe with thee
The germ of immortality!
And calm and peaceful shall I sleep,
Rocked in the cradle of the deep.
By Emma Hart Willard

Steamer *Coos Bay* alongside Pier, about 1809.
(Ventura County Historical Museum)

The sidewheel steamship *Commonwealth* - 1854.

THREE

GOLD RUSH STIMULATES COASTAL PASSENGER ERA

Trading along the California coast increased slowly until the goldrush days of 1849. After gold was discovered, a frenzy of shipping activity began in California. Hundreds of ships sailed around the Horn to San Francisco where the bay was filled with abandoned schooners and other sailing craft no longer needed. The demand for food and goods and vessels to ship them generated an active trade along the California coast and within the Santa Barbara Channel. At first sailing vessels, and later steamers, carried passengers, lumber, hardware, tallow and hides. Until piers or wharves were built into the sea from the various coastal communities, ships anchored at sea and lighters took passengers and goods ashore. Some of the Channel's most famous and colorful shipwrecks occurred during the period from 1850 to 1900 when most people and goods were transported along the coast by ships.

To speed up the trip to California from the East Coast, ships sailed from New York and other ports on the Atlantic Seaboard to Panama. Passengers went across the Isthmus by land to the Pacific side where they caught a ship to California. Around 1850 steamboats driven by sidewheels, called 'sidewheelers,' were entered into service from the East Coast to Panama and from Panama to California. The various shipping lines became very aggressive in trying to beat out their competitors.

Because of scheduling problems in the early years, passengers sometimes had to wait a month or two in Panama for a ship north to California. Many passengers ran out of money and were stranded in Panama.

Shipping Victims of Channel--1850 to 1900

As shipping trade increased in the Channel, vessel captains and their crews had to learn that the Santa Barbara Channel had unusual moods and could be dangerous. Many ship commanders did not learn fast enough.

The number of ship accidents and sinkings increased rapidly during the last half of the Nineteenth Century. Over 33 large ships were sunk from 1850 to 1900. While sailing vessels continued to have more accidents, 26 for the period, steamship sinkings increased to seven. Steamships were more maneuverable, but could not avoid accidents in the Santa Barbara Channel. Steamships crashed into Anacapa Island, Point Arguello (two times), Port Hueneme, Ventura Coastline (two times) and Santa Rosa Island.

Of the ships sunk, four were wrecked near Port Hueneme, seven near Ventura and four near Santa Barbara. The Islands claimed a large share of the wrecks, one at Anacapa, four at Santa Cruz, two at Santa Rosa and six at San Miguel. The rocky shore points claimed a few, one each at Point Conception, Point Arguello, Point Dume and Point Sal. Four met their fate by burning at sea. The wooden hulled ships were particularly vulnerable to fires due to their steam engines. Most of the ships were driven ashore in storms or ran aground in fog or foul weather.

The building of the wharves at Port Hueneme, Ventura and Santa Barbara brought ships closer to shore and increased the chances for serious accidents. Frequent collisions between ships and the wharves occurred in storms damaging the pier structures and ships severely.

Some of the ships wrecked were quite large. The *Crown of England,* a 1600-ton steamship, hit rocks at Santa Rosa Island and sank in November of 1894. The 365-ton wooden steamship *Yaquina* went ashore in the fog and was destroyed near Port Hueneme. Two four-masted sailing ships sank; the *Golden Horn* hit a reef in fog at Santa Cruz Island and the *King James* caught fire off Point Conception. The greatest known loss of life in a single shipwreck up to that time, 30 people, occurred when the *Yankee Blade* struck rocks at Point Arguello on September 1 of 1854. A minimum of 40 persons died and an unknown number were injured in the reported ship sinkings and shore wrecks from 1850 to 1900.

The *Winfield Scott* Goes Down

The *Winfield Scott*, built in 1850 in New York for passenger service, was a large wooden ship for its time, being 225 feet long, about 30-35 feet wide and weighing 1,291 tons. A very modern sidewheeler, it had two engines and a beautifully designed interior. While constructed for less, it carried as many as 375 cabin and 450 steerage passengers. After its launching October 27, 1850, the *Winfield Scott* was sent to the Pacific. Unfortunately, passengers had been waiting impatiently for some time at Panama for the *Winfield Scott*. In January 1853, the price of a ticket from New York to San Francisco by way of Panama ran about $305 for first cabin, $200 second cabin and $85 for steerage.[6]

On December 2, 1853, the *Winfield Scott*, under the command of Captain LeRoy left San Francisco for Panama with 375 cabin passengers, 450 steerage passengers, U.S. Mail, an estimated $2 million in bullion, and a lot of miscellaneous cargo. The ship was loaded with gold miners, many successful, who were leaving California to return to the East Coast.

While accounts by the shipping company and survivors differ somewhat as to what actually happened, events were as follows. The trip was uneventful until the ship entered the Santa Barbara Channel around 2:00 a.m. on the morning of December 4th. It ran into heavy fog in the vicinity of the Channel Islands. The officers were unable to take a bearing as their only means of navigation was dead reckoning (distance traveled in a given amount of time). Between two and three o'clock in the morning, without warning, the ship ran ashore at Anacapa Island. Fortunately, the ship did not sink immediately. The captain attempted to go astern but lost the use of the rudder. The ship was pushed into the rocks by the pounding surf. He then sent a boat along the Island shore to find a landing place. Upon return of the boat with news of a beach nearby, the captain commenced to unload the passengers.

Another ship, the *California*, came by on December 9, 1853, and was hailed by cannon fire from the *Winfield Scott*. A boat from the *California* took off all the women and children, but had no space for the men on the ship. The *California* was to suffer a similar fate in the Channel years later. The following day, the *Southerner* worked its way through heavy fog and landed provisions on the beach for the people remaining ashore. Another ship from San Francisco, the *Republic*, arrived and examined the *Scott's* situation. By this time, the ship's hull had been broken. All those remaining on the beach embarked on the *Republic*, along with the mail and other goods, and returned to San Francisco. The sea kept hammering away at the ship. Soon there was nothing visibly left of the ship. It was reported that Captain Le Roy of the *Winfield Scott* "died shortly after, broken-hearted."[7]

The *Winfield Scott* on her maiden voyage, 1852.

The shipping company which owned the *Scott* maintained great secrecy about the accident. It was almost three weeks after the accident before any stories were reported to the press. Many of these were third and fourth-hand from people or officers aboard.

Over 40 years later, on January 17, 1896, the Ventura Free Press published an interview with a passenger who survived the crash. The passenger, F. S. Crane of Sycamore, Illinois, visited Ventura to relive his experience and look at the location of the wreck. His account, told to reporter John C. Wray, describes graphically the confusion and events on board and on shore that had not been reported before:

> *April 14, 1853, in company with William Stolp and Willis Wright, now a resident of Stockton, Cal., I left Aurora, Ill., with 150 head of beef cattle which we intended to drive to the gold mines in California for market. After a drive across the plains lasting six months, we reached Hangtown, October 30th, with 110 head, having lost 40 head on the road. After disposing of my share in the venture I decided to return home by steamer, not caring to undergo the hardships of a back trip overland. My partners decided to remain in the gold fields and I left them behind and made my way to San Francisco, and took passage for New York on the* **Winfield Scott**, *Dec. 2nd. The cabin was full and I took a berth in the steerage with about 350 to 400 others, principally miners returning east, nearly all of whom had specie belts well filled. There were a good many hard characters among them and life for the first twenty-four hours was anything but pleasant.*

> *Everything went along all right until the afternoon of the 3rd, when a heavy fog set in, so heavy that you could almost cut it with a knife. By 11 o'clock that night everything was quiet and all lights out in the steerage as nearly everybody was tired out and sleeping. As nearly as I can fix the time, between 2 and 3 o'clock in the morning (the 4th) I felt a shock coupled with a grinding, crushing kind of noise, which woke me out of a sound sleep and feeling that some accident had happened, I jumped out of my*

bunk and ran for the deck, being one of the first, if not the first, of the steerage passengers to reach there. I found everything in confusion, and realized at once that we had gone ashore. The bow of the steamer was well up on a bank of some kind which could be seen indistinctly through the fog.

I went back to my berth, and had hard work in getting my shoes and coat which I had left behind when I made the first rush for the deck. The passengers had by this time become panic stricken, and were crowding over each other in their anxiety to reach the deck. The wildest kind of rumors ran through the ship, some declaring that the boilers had burst, others that we were sinking fast, but everyone was for himself, with no thought of anything but saving his life and his dust, if he had any. When I reached the deck the second time, probably three to five minutes had elapsed from the time I felt the first shock, I found that the steamer was fast on the rocks, and that she was settling gradually by the stern. The wildest kind of confusion prevailed, but Captain Le Roy and his officers, assisted by Captain Brown, a cabin passenger, were getting the panic stricken passengers quieted down and somewhat under control.

In about twenty minutes from the time the steamer struck the first boat was lowered, but not until the Captain and first mate had stood over the davits with drawn revolvers to keep the excited and frightened passengers back. The boat was manned by four of the crew and one of the mates, with instructions to find out how close the ship lay to land, and discover, if possible, a landing place for the boats. The boat came back in about five minutes and reported a safe landing close at hand, on what appeared to be an island. From remarks which I overheard afterwards I believe the Captain thought he was ashore on Santa Cruz Island.

As soon as the Captain was satisfied that a landing was possible he ordered the boats lowered, and the passengers *transferred to the shore. By this time the panic had subsided as the vessel remained fast on the rocks as though in a cradle, and the transfer was made rapidly and safely. The women, children and sick persons, of which there were quite a number, being first looked after. By daylight everybody was safe on shore, or what appeared to be the shore, but in reality was a rock lying close to the main island.*

With daylight the fog lifted and for the first time the officers knew where they were. A second landing from the rock to the Island was made and we went into camp for the eight days and a half which we were obliged to pass on the island. The first day a boat with four men was dispatched to the mainland with instructions to make their way overland to the nearest point from which word could be wired to San Francisco. We saw them start for the mainland, but never learned of their arrival.

The Captain and crew worked hard and got on shore nearly all of the mail matter, bullion and baggage, over which a guard was placed, as the rowdy element among the passengers began to manifest itself as soon as the first panic subsided, and before the passengers had been transferred to the land. An Irishman and a Negro were caught in the act of cutting open carpet bags in the cabin. They were ironed and carried ashore for trial. We immediately formed a vigilance committee and appointed a police patrol of the camp, with Capt. Brown as chief.

The two thieves were tried and an example made of them for the benefit of the rowdy element who showed a decided disposition to run things their own way. The two men were stripped, spread eagled on the sand and whipped by Captain Brown in person. Every time he brought the rope down he brought blood. It was a fearful spectacle but it had the desired effect, and no more rowdyism or thieving occurred. Our provisions were scanty; during the last two days we were forced to issue short rations, but everything considered we got along fairly well.

*The third day we sighted the Pacific Mail steamer **Illinois**, which sent a boat ashore, learned our condition and took one of our officers and a few passengers and left for San Francisco to send us succor. The morning of the 13th she returned and we were transferred, with bullion, mail and baggage, to Panama, without further incident of importance, but more than thankful for our deliverance from what at one time seemed certain death. For myself I never wanted any more ocean travel in mine and was glad when I set foot in New York City.*

Refuge on Richardson's Rock

A smaller but quite nefarious sinking took place in 1851 near Richardson's Rock. The tiny island, six miles northwest of San Miguel Island, is used to determine the State's three-mile offshore waters' boundary. Only a couple of hundred yards long, the U.S. Government uses it to mark the Channel Islands National Marine Sanctuary boundary. A haven for gulls, pelicans, seals and sea lions, it is covered above the wave line with a thick crust of bird guano that looks like a snowy crest from the sea. Mariners use the rock as a bearing when entering the Santa Barbara Channel from the west.

In 1851, Nathan Richardson, a bootmaker from Michigan who had struck it rich during the Gold Rush by selling boots to the '49ers,' was on a ship from San Francisco on his way to the East Coast to pick up his family. The vessel was carrying a shipment of gold from the booming gold fields and about 13 passengers.

In the words of Nathan's descendant, George Richardson of Visalia, California: "The second night out there was a big commotion aboard. The captain and crew opened the petcocks in the ship to sink it and set out in a longboat with the gold."

No one ever heard of the renegade captain and his men. "I hope they drowned," George said. Some passengers panicked, but a few, including Nathan, somehow made it to what is now Richardson's Rock. They couldn't have been there long because there is no way to survive on the island. They hailed a passing ship that took them back to San Francisco. It is not known exactly

Point Arguello, Graveyard of the Pacific

when the island was named Richardson Rock, but the charts so designate it and have for a century.

The *Yankee Blade* Disaster

On Saturday September 29, 1854, four steamers prepared to leave San Francisco for a voyage to the south. The *Yankee Blade*, a three-year-old ship, carried an estimated 819 passengers, 120 crew members and undoubtedly some stowaways. The *Yankee Blade* was bound for Panama and was rumored to be racing with the **Sonora**. The **Sonora** was also heavily loaded, carrying returning miners to the East by way of Panama. The captains of the *Yankee Blade* and the *Sonora* reportedly had wagered a $5,000 bet as to which ship would reach Panama first.[8] Of the other two steamers preparing to leave, the *Cortez* was bound for Nicaragua and the *Goliah* for San Diego.

Around four o'clock in the afternoon, the four ships let off a blast from their steam whistles, pulled up their gangplanks and headed out to sea. Captain Randall of the *Yankee Blade* reportedly slowed to allow the *Sonora* to reach him. When even, the *Yankee Blade* lowered its flag in a signal of challenge; the *Goliah* reciprocated, and the race was on. The *Yankee Blade* was owned by the Independent Opposition Line, a competitor of the *Sonora's* shipping line.

When the *Blade* ran into dense fog along the coast about 24 hours after leaving San Francisco, Captain Randall did not reduce speed or check the depth of the water near Arguello. He believed, as have many other captains, that he was farther out to sea. Randall kept his huge paddlewheels working at cruising speed. Unknown to him, a contrary current that had a strong inshore set had pushed him east toward shore in the vicinity of Honda. Randall thought he was south and clear of the mainland when he turned onto a course south for Panama. The *Goliah* wisely slowed down when it encountered fog near Point Arguello and the Santa Barbara Channel.[9]

The *Yankee Blade* hit the reef on October 1, 1854 running at full cruising speed about three-quarters of a mile offshore from Point Arguello. The ship had run more than 50 feet onto a rocky reef just south of Hondo's Bridge Rock. The forward part of the ship tilted upward and the aft portion went underwater.

The ship's officers and crew responded well at first and handled the disaster correctly. Women and children passengers were assembled near the lifeboats. The crew in the engine and boiler rooms acted promptly in preventing any boiler explosions. As to what actually happened next on board the *Yankee Blade,* accounts differ as in the *Winfield Scott* wreck. Because of the heavy surf running, confusion and chaos reigned during the lifeboat launchings. Several women were drowned while the first lifeboat was being launched. The after-tackle released accidentally, and the boat dumped some of its passengers into the sea. Shortly thereafter, another lifeboat with about 30 people aboard, including the first officer of the ship, was swamped when launched. Many miners, heavily weighted with their gold belts, drowned. An estimated 17 men and women lost their lives in the accident.

Captain Randall decided to go ashore on the next boat. He was successful in taking the lifeboat through the surging seas and loaded with passengers ashore. The two boats continued to bring load after load of passengers and crew ashore for the next six hours, until 150 to 200 passengers were finally landed.

With Randall and several of the officers gone, the crew on board became very disorderly and discipline was lost. Several of the crew members, with some of the steerage passengers, broke into the liquor storage room cabin and commenced to get drunk. Fortified with the alcohol, they practically took command of the ship. The crew stole from the passengers, opened bags and trunks, beat and threatened to murder passengers for their valuables. Many of the passengers, faced with the pounding waves on the ship and the marauding, drunken crew and stowaways, jumped overboard, making improvised life rafts, and tried to reach shore by their own means. Some made it, but many did not.

Around 10:00 p.m. that evening, Captain Randall and the Third Officer returned to the ship. By this time the First and Second Officers had disappeared. Due to the wind coming up and the waves increasing in size, the officers decided to keep the remaining passengers on board for the night. Randall's return helped settle the raucous conditions on board.

The next morning, now October 2, Captain Randall and his Third Officer resumed rescue operations. The boats were loaded with food and supplies and taken to shore for the passengers. Only about half the passengers had been landed by noon. While it was daylight, conditions were still somewhat foggy.

The *Goliah*, moving along slowly, luckily saw the wreck of the *Yankee Blade* about three-quarters of a mile offshore. The ship was prevented from sinking by a rock pinnacle that was about six feet below the surface of the sea. Captain Thomas Haley of the *Goliah* stopped his ship about a half-mile to sea from the *Yankee Blade* and immediately launched her lifeboats to the aid of the *Yankee Blade*. Those aboard the *Goliah* could hear the screams for help from people in the sea and people trying to escape the rampaging crew and passenger members. Four of the *Goliah's* boats, with the two boats from the *Yankee Blade*, took about 600 of the passengers on board their already heavily loaded ship.

The *Goliah* then went rapidly to San Pedro to land the passengers. Captain Haley lent Captain Randall about a dozen revolvers and ammunition to help keep order. Taking the guns ashore with him, Randall distributed them to responsible people, and some order was restored. The crew members, knowing that bullion estimated to be worth about $153,000 was stored aft, attempted to reach it. Fortunately, the bullion was underwater, therefore thwarting their goal.

The passengers on the beach assumed they had been saved but now faced another difficult situation. Some of the crew members, steerage passengers or stowaways grouped together and started beating and robbing the passengers on shore. The *Yankee Blade* pirates offered to sell their stolen food supplies and goods at unbelievably high prices to the stranded passengers.

The *Goliah* returned on October 8 to take the remaining survivors on board. By clever boat handling, all passengers on shore were brought aboard the *Goliah*. Altogether, in the transfer of crew and passengers from the *Yankee Blade*, about 30 lives were lost.

The behavior of the officers, crew and many of the passengers was unbelievably bad during the tragedy. In the maritime inquiry that followed the shipwreck, apparently no punitive action was recommended to be taken against Captain Randall's temporary desertion of the ship or the action of the crew and stowaways. One passenger's body was found with axe wounds about his head and his pockets turned inside out.

Captain Randall was severely criticized for running the *Yankee Blade* so close to shore, causing the wreck, and afterwards leaving the ship and losing control to crew members and rampaging passengers. He fared well in the end when an article appeared in a newspaper months later stating, "Captain Randall of the ship *Ada* has succeeded in recovering the treasure of the *Yankee Blade*, and his share would be in the neighborhood of $80,000."[10] Many of the dead from the wreck were buried on the cliffs above Point Pedernal, known locally as "Saddle Rocks."[11]

When Captain Randall returned to salvage the bullion, he had the assistance of the company insuring the *Yankee Blade*. He got the U.S. Navy to assist in salvage operations. Randall, with Lieutenant Cuyler, apparently recovered two boxes of bullion, a case of whiskey, and a passenger's suitcase. A Santa Barbara newspaper reported that Captain Randall said he did not think any more money could be recovered, due to the heavy swells rolling over the wreck.[12]

Captain Randall, however, did return about two months later and started diving operations again. He reportedly recovered four boxes of gold with an estimated value of $69,300. That amount was not turned over to the owners, however. Only about $35,300 was delivered. The owners, feeling they had been cheated, charged the three divers with stealing their money. The case never came to trial, as two of the men disappeared and one previously arrested was released on bail.

Channel Claims a Pathfinder

The first steamship to sail around Cape Horn to the Pacific Coast in 1848, the *California,* was totally wrecked in 1883 near Port Hueneme. The ship had served its company well for 35 years along the California coast and had helped other ships in trouble on numerous occasions.

Golden Horn: **An International Incident**

The four-masted, 1,842-ton British barque, *Golden Horn*, which was 286 feet long and had a beam of 40' 2," had made it from New South Wales with a 2,808-ton cargo of coal, when it hit the southwest side of Santa Rosa Island on September 12, 1892. The changing currents off the coast had put the *Golden Horn* a reported 50 miles off course. In the disaster, the crew of 28 men managed to board their lifeboats in time and rowed for 24 hours across the Channel to Santa Barbara and safety. The crew lamented that the ship's kitty was lost, but were glad that the ship's rats and flea stowaways were drowned at sea. Santa Barbarans very kindly supplied the crew with food, clothing and shelter.

Four young Santa Barbarans saw an opportunity to make some money from the *Golden Horn.* Aware of the salvage rights provided by international maritime laws, the men used a borrowed sailing boat to cross the 45 miles of fog-shrouded ocean to reach the stranded vessel. They worked frantically to salvage whatever valuables were aboard before the ship, whose copper-sheathed bottom had been torn by the rocks, broke up.

Three days later, while still loading salvage aboard their boat, the British Consul from Los Angeles pulled alongside and ordered the young men off the British-owned vessel. The young men, well aware of their salvage rights, refused to leave and told the consul and his staff to cast off.

As a British ship was in the Santa Barbara Bay, it was decided to hold a hearing on the shipwreck and the salvaging episode. A formal court of inquiry was established, formed by the British Consul, British captain of the *Arches* anchored at Santa Barbara and a British citizen. The Board exonerated the Captain because of the high seas, heavy fog and "strong northeast currents that set upon the southwest shore of Santa Rosa Island...are not referred to in the books of sailing instruction or charts, and since the Island is in direct route from Australia to San Pedro, mariners should be informed of it."

The maritime court of inquiry held also that the Santa Barbara salvagers were within the law and could sell their salvage and keep the proceeds. The *Golden Horn* was eventually battered to pieces by the waves and rocks of Santa Rosa Island.

First Pacific Ocean Tanker Destroyed

Needing another source of transportation for their increasing oil supply, Thomas Bard and his two oil company partners, Hardison and Steward, designed and built the first bulk oil tanker in the Pacific, the *W. L. Hardison*. It was a wooden-hulled steamer with auxiliary sails built to carry 6,500 barrels of oil in iron tanks from the production source in Ventura to San Francisco.

Hardison was given responsibility for the construction of the vessel. Bard instructed Hardison to have a ship built with an iron hull for safety reasons. Unfortunately, while Bard was in the east on a trip, Hardison contracted with a San Francisco firm for a wooden hulled ship. It was a mistake that did not make Bard happy. The ship only made seven voyages carrying oil before it caught fire and burned next to the Ventura Pier on June 25, 1889. While the ship was taking on crude oil, an inexperienced first mate lowered a lamp down to check on the level of oil in the tank. Luckily, no one was killed. Finding they needed more resources to accomplish their mutual goals, Bard, Hardison, and Steward formed an alliance with a third company and formed the Union

W.L. Hardison--First Pacific Coast oil tanker, 1889.
(Ventura County Historical Society).

W. L. Hardison Burning at Ventura Pier--June 25, 1889.
(Ventura County Historical Museum)

Oil Company in 1890. Richard Bard became the first President of the Company and continued in that role until he became a U. S. Senator in 1900.

Many other ships were to suffer the same fate near the Ventura wharf. At least 12 large ships went aground at Ventura in the 1800s and early 1900s. Some city streets near the wharf are named after the ships that were wrecked, including the *Lucy Ann,* (December 4, 1875); *Kalorama*, (March 1876), and the *Crimea* (April 1, 1876).

Shipwreck Skeletons a Problem

Some of the shipwrecks became a nuisance or interfered with shoreline development years later. The *Ocean King,* wrecked on the beach at Santa Barbara in June of 1892, had to be moved from its underwater grave 75 years later as it was in the path of a new outfall sewer being built out to sea from Santa Barbara. Another ship that sank almost a century ago near the Ventura wharf moved 100 feet in the 1960s, stopping on top of an underwater oil line.

Channel Wharf Construction

Fierce competition evolved between the different coastal cities in the Channel for the shipping market. Between 1871 and 1874, wharves were built at Port Hueneme, Ventura, Serena (between Summerland and Carpinteria), Santa Barbara (Stearns), More's Landing (near Goleta), Gaviota, Port of Lompoc, Point Sal (near Guadalupe) and Port Harford. Shipping by coastal ships was the primary method by which agricultural products and goods were shipped in and out of the Channel cities until the turn of the century.

Heavy coastal passenger and freight shipping continued until 1904, even though rail service was available from Los Angeles to Santa Barbara in 1887. After completion of the railroad from Los Angeles through to San Francisco in 1901, the railroad made sharp inroads into coastal shipping traffic. Sail and paddle ships were the major link to the outside world, however, due to the Basin's physical isolation for more than half a century.

The Port Hueneme Wharf was built in 1871 and was 900 feet long. It was extended 1,500 feet in 1880 to handle increased activity. During the year 1888, 169 steamers, 23 schooners, and

Sailing schooner approaching Hueneme Pier in 1895.
(Ventura County Historical Museum)

S.S. Pomona alongside Ventura Pier, 1895.
(Ventura County Historical Museum)

44 steam schooners for a total of 236 vessels used the wharf. For many years the wharf became the second largest grain shipping port between the Bering Strait and Cape Horn.

Stearns Wharf was built in 1872 and was 1,500 feet long, the largest wharf on the Pacific Coast at the time. Santa Barbara citizens predicted that Santa Barbara would be the shipping center of the West Coast. Santa Barbara and Port Hueneme Wharf advocates fully anticipated that they would compete successfully against the then small harbor of Los Angeles.

Stearns, Ventura, Port Hueneme, and other wharves were damaged often by storms and ships crashing into the piers. In a big storm in 1878, 900 feet of Sterns' 1,500-foot-long pier were destroyed. The wharf was repaired and extended to 2,500 feet in 1878 after a dispute with the city. Shortly after repairs were completed, the wharf was damaged again. On New Year's Eve of 1878, an unusual but wild typhoon swept through Santa Barbara. Accompanying winds and squalls from a Pacific typhoon brought driving rains and developed into Santa Barbara's most damaging waterspout of record.

The **Santa Barbara Weekly Independent** of November 20, 1885, reporting seven years after the event, said that the twister originated near Stearns Wharf and threw an anchored lumber vessel up against the wharf and into shore toward the warehouses that clustered at the foot of the pier. A Chinese junk near the origin of the spout was swamped and subsequently sunk before the gigantic waterspout came ashore. It dropped a torrent of water from its vortex, rolled on up De La Vina Street, its roaring whistle striking terror in the hearts of Santa Barbarans.

The snakelike twister uprooted sycamore and oak trees, pulled a barn from its foundation that slid up De La Vina for blocks until it finally disintegrated. A horse that had been in the barn was reportedly carried through the air for at least a block and then set down gently and safely. Surprisingly, only one death resulted from this unusual storm.

After the 1878 storm, Stearns repaired the damage more quickly. A small wharf had been built at the foot of Chapala Street a few blocks west of Stearns Wharf in the late 1860s. The southeast storm of 1878 destroyed the Chapala pier. After considering the cost of rebuilding and the competition from Stearns Wharf, the owners abandoned their structure.

Stearns Wharf continued as a major shipping facility until the mid-1920s. For years it handled on the average one passenger vessel a day and unloaded as much as 15 million feet of lumber in one year. The growth of the harbor at San Pedro and the construction of the coast railroad ultimately damaged the Santa Barbara and Ventura County shipping trade.

Need for Lighthouses

The numerous coastal shipping accidents caused a clamor for lighthouses at dangerous points. After joining the Union in 1850, California became eligible for permanent lighthouses to replace the primitive tree-top lanterns used for at least fifty years by the presidios along the coast to let ships know where they were in the dead of night.

Santa Barbara County was allotted lighthouses at Point Conception and at Santa Barbara Point on the Mesa. The beacon and light keeper's residence was completed in 1856 at Santa Barbara Point at a 180-foot elevation. The stationary oil-burning lamp was lit at dusk and extinguished at dawn each morning. The red light was visible for about 20 miles at sea. In 1921, the oil lamp was replaced by an electric lamp that revolved.

The lighthouse was destroyed in the June 29, 1925, earthquake and was not rebuilt. In its place, an automatic light was installed closer to the cliff where it still stands. The lighthouse keeper's house was eventually replaced by Coast Guard housing for the crew of the cutter stationed at Santa Barbara Harbor.

Anacapa light station on isolated rocky Anacapa Island is one of the most important beacons in the Channel. The light was not built until 1912, although requests for its construction started 56 years earlier. The lighthouse and living quarters, not presently used, are located on a wind-swept promontory above the rocky cliffs of the inhospitable island. A hoist is used to move supplies to the facilities. The lighthouse installation includes a light, fog horn and a radio beacon. A record fog in the Channel once kept the horn going for 28 straight days. The light is automatically operated from Port Hueneme.

1905 photo of Hueneme lighthouse, built 1874.
(Ventura County Historical Museum)

Hueneme lighthouse being moved by barge in 1940.

The original lighthouse at Point Hueneme was built by Thomas Bard in 1874. It served until the Port Hueneme Harbor was built in 1938. The old wooden lighhouse was put on a barge for later relocation, but remained there until it was dismantled in 1943.

Point Conception Light Station is well-known for its Fresnel lens. Made in France, the lens was brought around the Horn in 1854 to be installed. A kerosene lantern was used until electricity was wired to it in the 1920s. The light can be seen 18 miles. The original kerosene system is kept in working order in case of a power failure. The light has been important to sailors along the rough gale-swept coast since its first beam.

Santa Rosa approaching Ventura Pier, 1900.
(Ventura County Historical Museum)

45

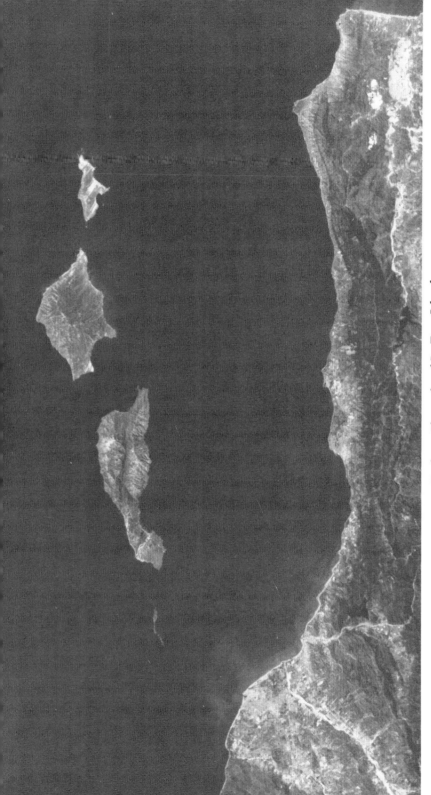

Santa Barbara Channel and Its Four Islands

FOUR

SHIPWRECKS AND DISASTERS
1900 TO WORLD WAR II

From 1900 to 1920, shipping along the coast increased, and so did the accidents. Thirty-one large ships were wrecked along the coast and the Islands or sank, one twice. The number of steamship sinkings increased to 14, but was less than the 18 sailing ships that went down.

Three of the steamers burned at sea, forcing their crews to abandon ship. The dreaded Point Conception-Point Arguello coastline claimed eight of the 31 wrecks and 48 of the 49 reported deaths. While sailing in rough seas off the coast, the cargo of the 2,354-ton steel steamer *Roanoke* shifted, causing the 276-foot ship to sink in 30 minutes. Only three crew members managed to survive and reach shore near Port San Luis on May 19, 1916. Captain Dickson and his wife both died in the sudden and strange accident. More than a thousand people were rescued from the 32 sinkings and wrecks.

Of the four ships that burned at sea, the helpful *Coos Bay* came to the rescue of the steamship *Berkeley* when it caught fire just east of Point Conception on November 29, 1907. The fire consumed the ship down to its waterline. The other three ships burned off Point Dume, Gaviota, and Summerland. The steamship *Rosecrans* burned to the water line off Gaviota after two of its tanks exploded. The ship was valued at $300,000 when it burned in September of 1912. Its hull, amazingly, remained afloat and was towed to San Francisco for salvage.

The Resilient And Restless *Coos Bay*

The *Coos Bay*, a passenger and lumber ship that had been a work horse for 37 years along the California coast, sank twice. The 544-ton steamship first went aground near the Ventura Wharf in January 1911 when her propeller broke while leaving the Ventura Wharf with a cargo of 2,000 sacks of beans. The helpless ship was carried by waves onto the beach. Her cargo of beans was removed and the ship lightened. With her prop repaired, the *Coos Bay* made her way to sea at high tide under power. The tough old ship was repaired and put back to work. The *Coos Bay* continued to be productive until December of 1914.

Prior to her sinking, the *Coos Bay* carried Klondike gold prospectors to Alaska and brought successful as well as not-so-fortunate miners back to Seattle. The Pacific Coast Steamship Company later switched her to a route between Portland and San Francisco. Her last coast run was between San Francisco and Ventura to the south. The *Coos Bay* helped many ships in trouble, rescued hundreds of people and was in many near-disasters herself before her final sinking.

As the *Coos Bay* approached the Ventura Wharf on a Saturday six days before Christmas in 1914 with her usual cargo, the captain did not realize until too late how shallow the water was next to the pier. As she was docking, the ship was bumped hard several times on the bottom by the rough seas. One particularly big wave pounded her so hard, the jolt severed her bow line to a buoy. The ship swung around sharply and smashed into the wharf. The *Coos Bay* sprang a leak and sank next to the pier. The huge swells continued to slam against her with the incoming tide. As if angry at her mistreatment, the ship repeatedly crashed into the wharf. By noon on the 19th, the *Coos Bay* had ripped a 200-foot-wide path into the wooden pier half way between shore and the wharf's end.

Salvage crews came from San Pedro and San Francisco to save her, but it was too late. The sunken vessel was bought by Robert Sudden, who sold her remaining undamaged cargo and dis-

The *Coos Bay* aground at Ventura, 1911.

Steamer *Coos Bay* ramming Ventura Pier, 1914.
(Ventura County Historical Museum)

mantled her, even removing her engine and boilers. In a few years, the drifting sands completely covered her skeleton.

As if to remind Venturans of her presence, the sea washed the sand away from her grave in 1927 and exposed her gaunt and worn grey skeleton. The sea covered her again. But in 1949, 35 years after her sinking, the *Coos Bay* decided to move one hundred yards, stopping on top of an oil line. For the *Coos Bay* to die in harness may have been better than rotting slowly in some neglected backwater area.

Santa Rosa Disaster

The 2,416-ton steamship *Santa Rosa* was a coastal workhorse like the *Coos Bay* and had her share of troubles. As the steamer approached the Santa Barbara wharf on the evening of September 25, 1885, Captain Johnson, normally a cautious seaman, seemed to lose control of the vessel. The bow plowed directly into the end of Stearns Wharf, breaking off the sturdy pilings and cutting through the heavy planking. The ship had so much headway that it smashed into the warehouse for over 50 feet. The light and unloaded ship's high-riding freeboard acted like a sail in the easterly wind and made the skipper lose control, causing damage to ship and wharf.

The *Santa Rosa's* service came to an end on July 7, 1911. While bound for San Diego from San Francisco, the steamer ran aground north of Point Arguello, at the west end of the Santa Barbara Channel. The ship struck rocks offshore before dawn, but for some unknown reason the captain permitted no evacuation until six o'clock in the evening. At that time, a delegation representing the 200 frightened and concerned passengers talked to the ship's officers. Plans were made to abandon ship.

The winds and seas were exceptionally high. Although several other ships stood by to attempt rescues, it was impossible to get lines aboard. Lifeboats and nets were used to get the passengers and crew off the ship. When the passengers engaged the pounding surf, all of the boats capsized. People were tumbled and smashed against rocks by the mountainous waves and strong tide. In the evacuation process, a dozen people lost their lives and over a hundred were injured, many seriously.

The *Santa Rosa* onshore at Point Arguello, 1911.

The ship broke in two as the captain went over the side. The center mast had fallen into the sea so that the forepart of the vessel was all that was visible above the surging seas. By the next day, it was clear that the Santa Rosa could not be salvaged. Parts of it washed up on to the rocky beach.

The *Aggie* Swells and Pops

The *Aggie,* a Norwegian five-masted, steel-hulled barque paid a strange but expensive price for taking a short cut between San Miguel and Santa Rosa Islands. On May 5, 1915, in heavy seas, the skipper of the *Aggie,* not realizing how dangerous the passage was, plowed onto Talcott's Reef and was held fast by the seas and reef. Water started seeping through the hull into the hold filled with grain. The grain swelled and expanded with such power that it slowly ripped the ship apart from stem to stern. The steel ship was totally destroyed, but its 18 crew members were rescued.

Great White Fleet Visits Santa Barbara

On April 25, 1908, 16 ships of the U.S. Navy, making up the Atlantic Fleet popularly known as The *"Great White Fleet,"* steamed into the Santa Barbara Channel and dropped anchor off the City's harbor. Headlined in the Morning Press as "Armada's Magnificent Spectacle as it Steamed into this Port," the Fleet was on its way around the world under orders from President Teddy Roosevelt to show the flag of our country.

The same paper stated that "Santa Barbara's most glorious day has been recorded in the pages of history. . . .never such spectacles witnessed by such enthusiastic crowds." A parade with 1,600 sailors of the Fleet dressed in white uniforms and carrying Springfield rifles marched along with thousands of Barbarenos on foot and on flower-decorated floats as they passed between the stand-line streets. Led by a bevy of flower girls, followed by the U.S. Marine bands of the four divisions of battleships, the spectacle has never been duplicated in the City's history.

The floral festival and parade was given in honor of the Fleet's Commanding Officer, Admiral "Bob" Evans and his men. President Theodore Roosevelt was present to receive the fleet in Santa Barbara. It was a big event for Santa Barbara. However, Admiral Evans did not review the parade. Rear Admiral Charles C. Thomas reviewed the fleet and parade instead. Admiral Evans became violently ill. His doctors had difficulty determining the cause of his illness, but suggested that the hot springs at Paso Robles might help him. The sick Admiral was put in a limousine and rushed to the baths at Paso Robles in adjoining San Luis Obispo County. It was his last trip. The baths didn't work and he died a few days later. Unfortunately, Admiral Evans died painfully as did Cabrillo, the Admiral of the first fleet to visit the Santa Barbara Channel 365 years earlier.

Sea Serpent Sighting In Channel

On November 28, 1901, the conductor on a Southern Pacific work train reported that he had seen a sea serpent at Punta Gorda along the Rincon in Ventura County. He and several other trainmen were standing on the beach when a monstrous sea serpent appeared in the breakers close to shore. The trainmen estimated that the creature was at least 40 feet long. Its head resembled an alligator, they said, and its wide jaws opened and closed below eyes that protruded from its gigantic head. The watching men ran in fear as the creature turned toward them, its baseball-sized eyes staring at them over the pounding surf. The monster disappeared, but reports indicated that a sea serpent had been seen at sea between Santa Barbara and the Channels Islands before.

FIVE

PASSENGER AND NAVAL SHIP DISASTERS 1920 TO 1940

Rising commercial activity coupled with population growth increased Channel traffic in the period from 1920-1940. A total of 44 vessels were reported destroyed by sinking (6), stranded or wrecked on shore (27), burning at sea (4), or foundering on rocks (6). Both commercial and recreational vessels were involved in these accidents that took a total of 48 lives.

A greater variety of vessels had accidents in the Channel than in the previous 20 years. Only six commercial sailing vessels were sunk compared to 37 motorized ships. More collisions were occurring. Three freighters and one yacht had ship-to-ship collisions. The vessels having accidents were getting larger. The passenger liner *Harvard* was 376 feet long and weighed 3,737 tons. Of the commercial sailing ships, the *James L. Stanford* was a four-masted barque weighing 970 tons.

The *Harvard* Hits a Reef

During the 1920s and 30s, many passenger ships ran between San Francisco and Los Angeles. The ships were very popular. Many businessmen preferred taking the ship rather than the train on their business trips. During the night of May 30, 1931, with the weather clear around 3:30 in the morning, the crew on duty of the *Harvard*, a 376-foot-long, 3,737-ton coastal passenger vessel, did not notice how close they were to Point Arguello. At cruising speed, the 25-year-old *Harvard* ran over an underwater reef 300 feet offshore opening a large section of the steamship's hull.

The quick-thinking Captain, Lewis B. Hilsinger, immediately sent out an SOS signal and, calmly and in an orderly manner, started evacuating the estimated 497 passengers. The ship was designed for 466 passengers. Many of the passengers took this for an adventure and continued to have a good time as they got into the lifeboats and abandoned ship. A U.S. Navy warship, the *U.S. Louisville,* was a short distance away and quickly responded to the *Harvard's* SOS. A nearby freighter, the *San Anselmo,* came in close to the *Harvard* and removed the passengers without incident. All of the nearly 500 passengers and 135 crew members were transferred safely to the battleship *Louisville.* Because the ship was lodged securely on the rocks, it was not in danger of sinking immediately, making it possible for the captain to get all the passengers off safely.

George Hilsinger, the son of Captain Hilsinger, recalled the tragic events the night the *Harvard* crashed into the rocks at Point Arguello. As an adult, he visited the accident site for the first time. He was six years old at the time of the accident. He said in an interview with the **Santa Barbara News Press** that, "I always wanted to see this spot." He said, "I can still remember my mother in tears, fearing my father's death." They didn't hear until the next day over the radio that Captain Hilsinger was safe.

George Hilsinger related, "I remember my father telling me that the only casualty was an unfortunate woman passenger who was bitten on the behind by a seal while attempting to board a lifeboat."

As a formality, the Captain was automatically suspended from duty as the ship's master for six months. Some of the officers and mates on duty at the time of the wreck were hit much harder. Several had their licenses suspended permanently for neglect of duty.

"Ironically, the night of the wreck of the *Harvard*, he (his father) was filling in for another captain of the company who was ill and couldn't make the run," George Hilsinger said. After the accident, Captain Hilsinger went to work as a port pilot for the Los Angeles Harbor Department. When the Second World War started he went on duty as an officer in the U. S. Navy. Interestingly, George also joined the Navy and saw his father in Saipan for the first time in three years.

Captain Hilsinger became a harbor pilot again after the war and continued in that capacity until his retirement at age 70. He died in 1970. A very creative and innovative person, he designed a new pilot boat which continued to be used years after his death.[13]

One person gained financially from the *Harvard's* disaster. Adam Sykes, who owned a ranch fronting the ocean near Point Arguello charged curiosity seekers fifty cents a car to park on his property and view the wreck. Fifty cents in 1931 was a lot of money. It is estimated that he parked from 20,000 to 30,000 cars while the interest was high to see the wreck of the *Harvard*.

The *Harvard* and its sister ship the *Yale* carried 368,777 troops between Southhampton and Le Havre during World War I. The popular *Harvard* carried thousands of passengers on the Atlantic and Pacific coasts before its unfortunate accident.

Many theories evolved as to why the *Harvard* was so far off course, including a reported "mysterious coast phenomenon," a "radio dead spot," a "strong inshore current," "drunken crew members," and "weather conditions." Others thought if was "faulty steering" and "unskillfulness." The blame was put on on-duty officers and crew members and not on the Captain, who was not on duty at the time. Evidence showed crew members altered log books to conceal that the *Harvard* was sailing too close to shore. Whatever the real reason for the accident, the treacherous currents, the sea and wind conditions at the entrance to the Santa Barbara Channel played a role in the disaster.

U.S. Naval Squadron Victim of Channel Forces

At the end of successful summer naval maneuvers in the Pacific, a fleet of 30 U.S. warships steamed out of San Francisco to their home base in San Diego on September 8, 1923. Spirits were high when the fleet steamed out of San Francisco. The officers and crews had been entertained at numerous parties, dinners and dances during Fleet Week, and were looking forward to returning to their home base in San Diego. Destroyer Squadron 11, part of the fleet, consisted of 14 destroyers.

The destroyers had been constructed during World War I and were the latest and best designed in the U. S. Navy. These 314-foot-long destroyers had a beam of 32 feet, a displacement of 1,250 tons and a draft of almost 10 feet. Each destroyer had two high-powered and two low-powered turbine engines that totalled 27,000 horsepower. Their two props could drive them at a speed of 32 knots. Each destroyer normally carried a crew of 114, but, due to post-war budget problems, carried a crew 20 to 30% smaller. The report of a subsequent Naval Court of Inquiry tells the story of the fleet's fateful encounter with the Channel.

The commodore of Squadron 11, Captain Edward H. Watson, had been given orders by the Commanding Officer of the Destroyer Squadrons, Admiral E. W. Kitelle, to maintain a full 20-knot speed for the San Francisco-San Diego trip of about 430 miles. Captain Watson was a highly respected Naval Academy graduate who had served as Captain of the Battleship *Alabama* during the First World War and had assignments as U.S. Naval Attache at the American Embassy in Tokyo, Japan, and other interesting duties. His father was a retired Rear Admiral.

Because of the endurance drill conditions given to them, Squadron 11 left after the bulk of the fleet. Watson, in his ship, the *Delphi,* led the destroyer squadron of 14 ships in three columns. Each ship in the column was to maintain a distance of only 150 yards between the stern of the preceding ship and its own bow. With darkness, a light fog set in along the coast. The destroyers continued to maintain their 20-knot speed. As the ships neared the Santa Barbara Channel, the fog became more dense.

Each destroyer had a navigator, but the orders of the Chief Navigator on the *Delphi* were to be followed by all ships. Their orders were to follow the lead of the *Delphi* and stay in close formation in the column. No radar was available to ships in 1923. Some radio navigation facilities were available, but many naval officers held little faith in the new radio equipment or radio directional finder (RDF) stations onshore. Captain Watson, LCDR Donald T. Hunter, the Commanding Officer of the *Delphi,* and LT (JG) Blodgett, technically the navigational officer on the *Delphi,* plotted their course by "dead reckoning." An RDF Station was located on Point Arguello and was in operation as Squadron 11 neared the Santa Barbara Channel in the evening. The Squadron had been on a south compass course.

At 8:30 in the evening, the officers on the *Delphi* planned to turn east after passing south and clearing Point Arguello. The dead reckoning position the officers plotted on their chart indicated that the *Delphi* was south of Point Arguello and about 12 miles out to sea. The *Delphi* commanding officer mistakenly thought that if the squadron continued any longer on their southerly course, they would run aground on San Miguel Island.

The *Delphi* took a radio bearing from the Point Arguello RDF Station. The bearing indicated that the *Delphi* was still north and just offshore of Point Arguello. The bearing was determined later to be accurate. Watson and Hunter, however, did not believe the radio station's bearing, trusting their "dead reckoning" position and calculations.

Some confusion occurred on the bridge during this period as signals were being received from the freighter *Cuba* which had run aground at San Miguel. The *Cuba* was sending SOS signals and rescue ships were in close radio contact with the *Cuba*, cluttering up the radio airwaves. The co-mingling of distress signals caused some confusion to the navigators.

Another radio bearing was received from Point Arguello Station which still placed the Squadron north of Arguello and closer to shore than their plotted position indicated. Blodgett, who believed in the radio direction finder system said to his two senior officers, "The bearings have been erratic by a few degrees, Captain, but they have all put us north of the Point. How about slowing for a sounding, Sir?"

Commodore Watson and Captain Hunter exchanged glances, and Watson said, "No, not much use--probably can't reach bottom--spoil our engineering run."[14] For lack of faith in a new radio navigational aid, not wanting to spoil a formation pattern, and not respecting the forces in the Channel, the men of Destroyer Squadron 11 were about to face disaster.

Convinced that the destroyers had passed south of Point Arguello, Watson and Hunter ordered their course changed a few minutes before 9:00 p.m. to an east course of 95 degrees, the normal compass course that would take them through the Santa Barbara Channel. As they changed course, the fog thickened considerably. The Captain continued to hold a speed of 20 knots.

Without any warning, the *Delphi*, being the lead ship, struck the shore first at full cruising speed. It was 9:05 p.m. The ship scraped the bottom gently and then hit the rocks with a head-on crash, stopping immediately. The *Delphi* crew were thrown about the ship in terrible disorder.

Captain Watson, still not realizing his true position, thought he had hit San Miguel Island 23 miles to the west. He quickly sent a message to the other ships, attempting to warn them away from

U. S. Destroyer aground at Honda, 1923.

The Destroyer *Nicholas* (311) at Honda.

the rocks. Unfortunately, he radioed the ships to "keep clear to westward, make 90°." He only made matters worse. He ordered them to turn more directly into shore.

The *Delphi* had actually hit the mainland at an area known as Honda, a few miles north of Point Arguello. Seeing that the *Delphi* was sinking, Hunter ordered the ship abandoned. The other destroyers, only 150 or so yards behind each other, had little time to change course or stop. Many of them frantically put their engines in reverse, but not in time.

The destroyer *S. P. Lee,* astern of the *Delphi*, put its engines full astern but had slowed only to eight knots before slamming into the rocks next to the *Delphi.* At about two-minute intervals, the *Nicholas, Woodbury, Young, Chauncey,* and *Fuller,* following trustingly astern of their Commodore, sickeningly crashed into the vicious, rocky coastline. The fog was so thick along the shore the ships could not see each other.

Fortunately, the other destroyers in the Squadron, listening to the calls and warnings and being a little suspicious of the dead reckoning of the lead ship, had slowed, pulled back, and gone into reverse in time. Even with their quick thinking, both of them touched bottom and one was damaged slightly in maneuvering out of the rough seas and rocky surroundings.

Eye Witness Account Of Tragedy

Eugene Dooman, foreign service officer on board the *Delphi* as a passenger and a friend of Captain Watson, described the crash in this account:

> *It was about 8·30 at night when Watson and I finished dinner. I sat on the window seat with my back to the to the bow, Watson facing me across the table. A rating came in with the message that Watson was needed on the bridge. He was away perhaps 20 minutes. As he sat down again at the table, he said that he had given orders to change course. Some moments later, I heard a grating sound, as though the ship had scraped bottom, and then immediately came the crash, the ship stopping instantly. I was thrown against the glass at my back, and Watson against the table. Drawers flew out of cabinets, and there seemed to be an explosion of paper and everything else movable. As Watson dashed out of the cabin, the ship's sirens sounded and searchlights came on. I also ran out on deck. The searchlights were on the second ship, which in a second or two crashed.*
>
> *It also sounded its siren and searchlights joined with those of the **Delphi** in lighting up the third ship. And so it went, ship after ship, each ship in line as it struck seemed to have turned more to the right than its predecessors, and one had turned enough to catch a rock on its right quarter, its headway operating to turn it slowly over on its side. Men could be seen climbin up the sloping deck and onto the ship's side as it turned over. There was considerable scurrying to and fro on the **Delphi**, with men rushing to their stations or running for lifebelts. It seemed to be a systematic and organized business, as evidenced by a lad bringing me a lifebelt. I decided I could be most helpful by keeping out of the way, so I headed for the Commodore's cabin to wait there until word came to abandon ship.*[15]

The grounded ships twisted and turned in crazy turmoil on the rocks and pounding waves. The *Young* turned over, trapping 20 men below. The officers and men aboard all the ships responded quickly and efficiently to the horror they now faced.

Because the rear echelon destroyer commanders did hold back and did not steer a 90° course into the rocks as ordered, they saved their ships. However, the captains who did follow orders, saw their destroyers become part of Arguello's "graveyard" of ships.

A Southern Pacific Railroad foreman, John Giorvas, who lived nearby in a company house, had looked out his bedroom window before going to bed and had seen flashes of light. Opening his bedroom window, he listened, heard some noises and went down the mesa to the coast to investigate. Almost in disbelief, he witnessed the destroyers twisting in agony in the sea. Learning of the disaster, Giorvas quickly called to nearby railroad workers on the plateau above Honda, who rushed to the shore to help the crewmen. The foreman quickly sent messages out and rescue parties were on their way. Help, including a doctor, came from Lompoc, a small community to the north of the area. Rescuers also came from Santa Barbara and from nearby ranches, including

The *Chauncey* (296) dropped anchor for the last time.

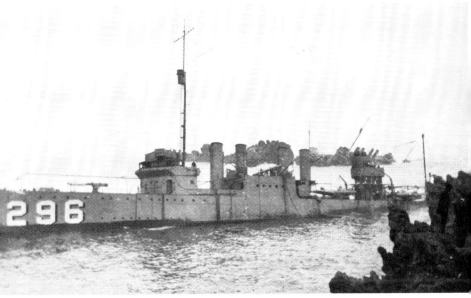

a woman by the name of "Ma" Atkins, the wife of a Southern Pacific telegrapher at Surf, five miles north of Honda.

A total of 800 officers and men were aboard the seven ships. During the night about 450 of the men got ashore, many with serious injuries. The nearby train track was used to transport survivors to Santa Barbara and San Luis Obispo hospitals.

Several fishermen discovering the disaster, used their boats, courageously maneuvering in and out of the rough seas to rescue the crew. The fishermen after rescuing the men, calmly went back to fishing without giving their names to any of the people they rescued. First aid, blankets and food were rushed to the scene. By the next day, the remaining officers and men made it to shore or were taken aboard rescuing ships. In a roll call it was determined 23 men were dead or missing in the disaster. Scores were injured.

The Navy estimated that the loss of the seven destroyers totaled around $13,500,000. In the attempted salvage work, no bodies were found in the wreckage of the destroyers. Ultimately, a total of 17 bodies were recovered. The bodies of six men were never found. The Navy did recover about 80 torpedoes valued around $5,000 each at that time, guns, and other equipment.

Visitors poured in from nearby areas to view the tragedy from shore. Most of them came by train, but roads were also jammed by vehicles trying to reach the scene.

A hex must have been put on the area. A few days later on September 12, 1923, the U.S. Navy battleship *Texas* collided with a steamer, the *Steel Seafarer*, 14 miles north of Point Arguello.

The Navy, shocked and embarrassed by the grounding of the destroyers, ordered an inquiry but tried to keep the disaster a secret. The press, of course, heard about the tragedy and forced the Secretary of the Navy to open the court of inquiry to the public.

Court Martial Held

A court martial was ordered for 11 officers, including Watson and Hunter. Charges of culpable inefficiency in the performance of duty were made against the officers. Although ordered to follow their lead ship, some of the squadron's skippers were charged with being derelict in their duties for not questioning the navigator's instructions from the *Delphi*. Many of the officers felt they were "damned if they did and damned if they didn't." It was made clear to them from the start of the voyage that they were not to interfere with the radio navigational communication of the *Delphi* or to break out of their close formation.

Captain Edward Watson and LCDR. Donald Hunter were found guilty of culpable inefficiency and negligence. LT (JG) Lawrence Blodgett was found not guilty of negligence as charged, but the verdict was set aside by reviewing Admiral Robinson. The other destroyer commanders were found not guilty of negligence as charged, but the Navy Judge Advocate General and the Secretary of the Navy, in reviewing the verdicts, disapproved of their not-guilty verdicts. This left a cloud over their future advancement and promotional opportunities in the Navy. Watson was given a reduction of 150 numbers on the promotional list and Hunter a loss of 100 numbers on the list. They would never be promoted again.

Captain Watson later served as Assistant Commandant of the 14th Naval District at Pearl Harbor, Hawaii until 1929 when he retired. He died in 1942.

The commanding officer of the *Delphi*, LCDR Donald Hunter, served as navigator of the battleship *Nevada*, as first lieutenant of the *Oklahoma*, and as an instructor at the Naval War College. He retired in 1929 and died in 1948. Hunter instructed at the Naval Academy for two years prior to his command on the *Delphi*.

Destroyer commanding officer William Calhoun did continue his career, establishing a very impressive naval record. Calhoun's ship had lost about 20 men. In the court martial, while relating what happened, he tried his best to keep composed, but choked up at the description of the lost men that he knew. Fortunately, his excellent leadership prevented more of his men from being killed in the disaster. Calhoun received a letter in December 1923 from Admiral Lewis Bayly of the Royal Navy who, reading of the Honda tragedy, wrote him:

> *It is a story of calm courage, perfect discipline and faith in God, and has done me a very great deal of good to read it. I like so much the order to 'be ready' to abandon*

ship. Some would have abandoned her and lost their lives. I hope an Englishman would have given the order you did: an American did it. The discipline must have been as near perfect as could be; everyone trusting in you and waiting for your order and then to thank God publicly for his rescue. Thank you for your splendid example. Yours sincerely, Lewis Bayly--very well done.[16]

Commander Calhoun commented at the court martial on Captain Watson's action at the tragedy: "I only hope that if ever I am faced with the tragedy that faced him that night, I'll be half the man that he was--cool, calm, courageous and thoughtful; never missing an opportunity to aid."

Calhoun served in the Navy for 44 years. He was in charge of Logistic Support of the Pacific Fleet and Naval Shore-Based Establishments in the Pacific Area during World War II. He retired in 1946 as a four-star admiral.

Destroyer Captain Roesch, asked years later about his conviction, said:

I believe my conviction was because I stated that I was following the leader, as of course was everyone else. I kept track of the navigation as well as possible, but we had nothing to go on but dead reckoning. We couldn't take soundings, and we were forbidden to ask for radio bearings. Anyhow, when my conviction was disapproved and all of the acquittals were disapproved, we were all in the same boat. The principal effect of these reversals was that all the skippers were put in the position of having been responsible for the loss of their ships.[17]

Retired Naval Reserve Captain Robert Kallman, co-author, recalled that when he was a midshipman during World War II, one of the destroyer commanders at Honda was his commanding officer. The officer related with great bitterness to the midshipmen how badly he and the other destroyer commanders had been treated by the Navy when they had only been following orders at the time of the tragedy at Honda.

The officers and crew of the seven destroyers performed admirably in the evacuation of the ships. No cowards existed on the seven ships that fateful night. The men courageously helped each other from the damaged and sinking ships onto the treacherous rocks during the stormy night. Many commendations were given to the officers and men for their skill in helping survivors ashore. It is amazing that only 23 casualties occurred under the circumstances.

Factors Contributing To Naval Grounding

Prior to the time the seven destroyers went aground, the liner *Cuba* ran aground at San Miguel Island. The captain of the *Cuba* claimed that there had been a mysterious change in the normal ocean current along the coast of California. The *Cuba* had been sailing northward to San Francisco. He claimed that an unusual current had moved him southward and east of his plotted position, forcing him to run aground at San Miguel. In the fog, he could not see the island until it was too late.

On September 9, 1923, newspapers in Los Angeles reported that strange sea and air currents along the coast had caused the U.S. Navy destroyers to be off course and run aground. Captain Knudsen of the steamer *Raymond* also stated upon reaching San Francisco that he had met very unusual and unexpected currents that had a southeasterly, inshore set.[18]

A few days prior to the tragedy, on September 1, 1923, one of the greatest known earthquakes occurred in Japan. It was claimed by many that the tidal waves and energy transmitted by the quake affected the ocean currents and wave action at the time the destroyers went aground along the California coast. The Japanese quake caused death to 143,000 people and injured thousands more.

Gin Chow's Forecasts of Japanese Earthquakes

On December 23, 1922, Gin Chow, a Santa Barbara County resident, posted a paper on the Santa Barbara Post Office which stated, "From 1924 to 1983, world in great trouble. Earthquakes come in September 1923 in Japan and Santa Barbara on June 29, 1925." True to his forecast, on September 1, 1923, a disastrous earthquake did hit Tokyo. The earthquake very well may have changed the currents in the Santa Barbara Channel and contributed to causing the worst U.S. Naval peacetime disaster in history. On June 27, 1925, the worst earthquake in Santa Barbara's history occurred, severely damaging the whole City.

Gin Chow forecast other weather phenomena that made him a celebrity and renowned person for years later.

The Kamoi Report

A year and a half later, a strange event occurred near the shipwreck location of the *Orowatti*. A Japanese Navy tanker, the *Kamoi*, reported by radio that it heard a ship calling for help off Pt. Sal, near where the *Orowatti* and the seven destroyers had gone aground in 1923. Several ships responded to the signal and sped to the location given by the *Kamoi*. The *Kamoi* nearly ran aground herself speeding to the rescue, reporting she was "hearing a steam siren blowing a distress signal." The arriving ships could find no vessel in the vicinity or in distress. The American steamship, *Tanana*, reported that the *Kamoi* must have seen the tanker, *Orowatti*, still stranded ashore. The unexplained distress signals must have come from the anguished cries of the destroyers, still breaking up in the breakers, or the floundering *Orowatti*.

Perhaps the lives and careers of several naval officers and men might have been very different if the destroyers in Squadron 11 had left San Francisco a day earlier or a day later and avoided the possible impact of the Tokyo earthquake on the currents near the Santa Barbara Channel.

Spray **Capsizes**

One of the worst sea disasters in the thirties happened on Sept. 24, 1939, when the fishing boat, *Spray*, got caught in a sudden, fierce, but not unusual, storm in the Channel. The *Spray's* captain returned to the wharf at Pt.Mugu to seek shelter and moor his boat, but the dock had been destroyed by the angry winds and seas. In attempting to turn the *Spray* around near the wharf, the boat was hit by huge waves and capsized. Of the twenty-four drowned, only two bodies were ever found.

An Unusual Rescue

Numerous small outboard motor boats are saved or aided by larger boats in the Channel every year. A reversal of the pattern occurred in August of 1927. Two men on a 38-foot cabin cruiser from San Pedro had attended a regatta at Santa Barbara and were returning home when their engine stopped running in mid-Channel. Two boys in a self-made 14-foot motor boat came across the drifting and helpless craft. Offering them a tow, the cruiser's owner quickly threw them a line.

On shore the family and friends of the two boys were organizing a search party around nine at night, when out of the fog loomed the 14-foot boat with the 38-foot luxury yacht aft of them Both boat crews were lucky the Channel was in a good mood.

The *Chehalis* aground at Point Conception, May 1933.

Great White Fleet at Santa Barbara, 1908.

Marijuana plants captured by deputies and police in
Oxnard, 1924. (Ventura County Historical Museum).

Ocean

Roll on, thou deep and dark blue ocean--roll!
Ten thousand fleets sweep over thee in vain;
Man marks the earth with ruin; his control
Stops with the shore; upon the watery plain
The wrecks are all thy deed, nor doth remain
A shadow of man's ravage, save his own,
When for a moment, like a drop of rain,
He sinks into thy depths with bubbling groan,
Without a grave, unknelled, uncoffined and unknown.

By Lord Byron

SIX

PROHIBITION SMUGGLING
AND RUMRUNNING

The enactment of the Volstead Act in 1920 changed America and generated smuggling activities in the Santa Barbara Channel. The Los Angeles area, with a big population, soon became a target for illegal liquor smuggling. Large quantities of liquor from Scotland, Canada, and other countries were shipped by boat to southern California. Few safe hiding places existed off the Los Angeles coast for smugglers to hide while waiting for a shore rendezvous. The Channel Islands Basin in Ventura and Santa Barbara counties provided an ideal base of operations. The four islands had numerous secluded coves only 12 to 30 miles off the mainland. Many isolated beaches and inlets along the coast of the two counties were ideal for shore deliveries. From the shore liquor could be driven to Los Angeles in only an hour or two.

With the advent of Prohibition, hard liquor escalated in popularity. Speakeasies, bootleggers and cocktails became the talk of the day. People who had never considered drinking were attracted to the cabarets and clubs where alcohol was available. For many, the prospect of patronizing the password-guarded 'speakies' represented the ultimate thrill.

People of the Channel Islands Basin were no exception. Wherever you went along the coast of the Channel the favorite drink was a mixture of 'hootch' and Nehi lime soda. Not only did people who hadn't been interested in drinking when it was legal, take it up, but people sought ways of making their own liquor. The production of home brew, whiskey, gin, and wine was soon a national pastime.

Patrolling the more than 150 miles of coastline in Ventura and Santa Barbara counties for seagoing rumrunners by law enforcement agencies was a difficult, if not impossible, task during Prohibition. The coastline is a series of remote beaches and sheltered coves interspersed between miles of rugged cliffs and rocky outcroppings. Literally hundreds of places were available to the overseas rum fleets to bring their goods ashore.

To enforce the Volstead Act in the 1920s, it took six different law enforcement agencies. A large segment of the public disapproved of the law and resisted its enforcement. One oldtimer in Ventura reported, "You didn't have any trouble getting what you wanted in Ventura County." The same was true in Santa Barbara County.

The Santa Barbara County Sheriff's Department maintained active surveillance at Gaviota and Refugio Beaches, as well as patrols at Naples, Goleta, Hendry's Beach (now Arroyo Burro), Santa Barbara Harbor, Montecito, and Carpinteria. In spite of these efforts, countless loads of illicit liquor were landed on Channel beaches during the 13 years of Prohibition.

In Ventura County, the remote beaches near Point Mugu, the Rincon, and Ventura were favorite locations for landing illegal liquor. One man walking along the Pierpont Bay beach one night during the 1920s was challenged by a man standing in the surf, who said, "What are you doing here?" "Just going for a walk," he answered. Assured that he was not a policeman, the man asked, "Do you want a job?" After a short discussion he was put to work loading barrels of whiskey from the beach onto waiting trucks.

Smugglers often used the then isolated Faria Beach on the Rincon (a few miles west of Ventura) to bring in illegal whiskey. Virginia Baptiste, daughter of Manuel Faria, recalled as a child seeing boats at sea blinking red lights to shore late at night. She said, "We never dared go near the beach when the lights were seen." Occasionally bottles of whiskey, buried in the 1920s are still found in the sand when foundations are dug for new houses.

With Los Angeles the big market and ultimate destination of most of the bootleg booze, movement of the liquor from the Channel beaches to the highway was the most critical part of the smuggling operation. Rum boats customarily anchored as close as possible and small boats, launched through the surf, ferried liquor between the rum runner and the beach. In Los Angeles, the bootlegging syndicates took charge of the illegal cargo. All sorts of cover vehicles--gasoline tankers, fertilizer trucks, trailers, buses, and private automobiles--were used to move the liquor down the coast. Traveling mainly at night and using diverse routes, the bulk of the fleet of vehicles made it through attempted barricades and police patrols to serve the thirsty population of the City of the Angels.

One truck and trailer could carry up to $500,000 worth of liquor. The payoffs to local property owners for allowing passage and storage on their land were enormous. One farmer in Goleta was offered a small fortune in cash for every day he allowed a load of booze to be hidden in his barn until it was picked up and delivered to a Los Angeles bootlegger.

Deputy Jack Ross, who years later became Santa Barabara County Sheriff, told the story of a bogus Richfield Oil tank truck that was discovered hidden in a grove of trees near Ellwood. Young Ross observed the truck being moved out at night and discovered that it was rendezvousing with boats unloading kegs at Eagle Canyon beyond the present Embarcadero subdivision. He watched the kegs being emptied into the tanker and arrested the trucker on the highway below Santa Barbara as he headed down the coast toward Los Angeles.

Bootleg liquor was often smuggled along the Channel in the false bottoms of fishing boats with fish piled on top of the cases of spirits. A line of ships called "Rum Row," loaded with liquor, often waited outside the territorial limit to sell their wares to small boat operators to bring ashore. Scotch sold at the ship for $50.00 a case and fetched $25.00 a quart ashore.

Low, fast speedboats were often used to land contraband at remote coves along the coast. Arroyo Burro, (Hendry's Beach), was one of the favorite spots. Trucks met the small boats at the

Bootlegger's apparatus seized in raid by Ventura authorities in 1922. (Ventura County Historical Museum)

arroyo where cargo was quickly transferred to the vehicles and the rumrunner paid off. Most of the smugglers felt safe since the average citizen usually turned his back on their activities.

Other rumrunners used to wait off Stearn's Wharf until darkness fell and everyone had left the pier. The ships would slip in without lights, heave to at the end of the wharf and quickly transfer liquor to a fleet of trucks. The land fleet would head south to arrive at their warehouse destinations before dawn.

Because of its central location, Prisoner's Harbor on Santa Cruz Island was a favorite anchorage for rum boats waiting to make their rendezvous with bootleggers on the mainland. Smuggler's Cove was also used, as it is today for drug smuggling. The high demand for liquor quickly exceeded the supply available from smugglers. The moonshiners came into a period of windfall profits that exceeded the infamous oil barons' highly publicized rake-offs. By the early 1920s, Santa Barbara and Ventura County moonshiners were producing whiskey for less than a dollar a gallon and selling it to bootleggers for almost forty dollars. Some of them held other jobs as protective covering, but most of the Channel's best-known still operators were quite open about their activities.

The gambling ship, *Miss Hollywood*, anchored beyond the three-mile limit off Stearn's Wharf, was a constant thorn in the side of law enforcement. Water taxis, loaded with gamblers from throughout the south coast, came and went with impunity, using the loading ramp of the then privately owned wharf. Many a passenger boarded the ship with an empty silver flask in his hip pocket, only to return ashore with his flask filled from the ship's ample supply of bootleg liquor. Small boats, leaving the harbor or launched through the surf of nearby beaches, would pull up to the seaward side of the brightly lighted vessel where an exchange of money and booze would take place.

In the early 1930s, the *Miss Hollywood's* business dwindled because of a series of editorials in the **Santa Barbara Daily News** denouncing the vessel's presence in the Channel. She finally left the area and relocated off the Los Angeles coast.

Rumrunner Cache found In Ventura County

In early October of 1925, several men hunting along the shore east of Port Hueneme came across 130 barrels of alcohol containing 50 gallons each. Apparently rumrunners had been towing the barrels of alcohol to a landing spot on shore when the barrels broke loose in rough seas or were abandoned to avoid detection. The barrels were made in England. The alcohol was valued at about $70,000.

A controversy soon evolved over the barrels recovered from the beach. Authorities claimed that by the time they saw the barrels on the beach the next day, 90 of the 130 remained. By the time Sheriff Robert Clark's deputies recovered the barrels and took them to the County Courthouse garage for safekeeping, only 72 barrels remained. The sheriff's men were questioned about the disappearance of the barrels. Hijackers reportedly took some of the missing barrels during the night before the sheriff moved them. The sheriff claimed that only 66 barrels, not 72, were actually taken to the courthouse. The public wondered who was taking the whiskey. The sheriff reported that someone rolled several barrels in the sand and lifted them into trucks at the location the alcohol was found. Sheriff Clark was the Grandfather of William Clark, President Reagan's former Secretary of the Interior.

Ventura County Sheriff Clark and men with whiskey found on
Hueneme Beach, 1925.(Historical Museum photo)

The Los Angeles Customs Office took the barrels recovered from Port Hueneme to Los Angeles and sold them to hospitals and wholesale drug companies. There was no report on how many were actually sold.

Battle With Coast Guard

The Coast Guard frequently intercepted suspected smuggling boats and chased them around the Channel. On October 18, 1926, spectators lined the shore between the Miramar Hotel and Summerland as a Coast Guard cutter pursued a fast rumrunner down the coast. Some time earlier, a long, low motor boat had pulled up to the wharf at the hotel, where it remained for about ten minutes without anyone disembarking. Just as employees of the Miramar began to wonder about the strange craft, a warning shout from a man aboard the boat alerted the crew that a Coast Guard cutter was approaching the wharf.

The motorboat gunned its engine and headed southeasterly with the cutter in pursuit. As the two boats raced along the coast, the cutter's crew opened fire near Summerland. Eyewitnesses reported that over 100 shots were fired by the cutter and that the water around the fleeing boat was spattered with near misses. The rumrunner's speed was estimated at 40 miles an hour, which took it out of range of the cutter's guns within a few minutes.

The cutter had been lying off Stearn's Wharf for at least two weeks, cruising occasionally around the Channel looking for illegal landings of liquor. Sheriff James Ross stationed his deputies along the coast that night to wait in vain for the rumrunner to try and land his cargo on the coast. It was believed that the cargo of bootleg spirits was probably offloaded instead somewhere along the Ventura coast.

Opium Smuggling

On September 17, 1910, the U.S. revenue cutter *McCullough*, commanded by Captain Daniels tied up at Stearn's Wharf in Santa Barbara. Ordered to the Channel to investigate reports of opium smuggling by local fishermen, the cutter's crew made a thorough search of every cave and cove on the four Channel Islands in the following days. Authorities suspected that a base camp existed on one of the islands where fishing boats could pick up opium to bring into the harbor.

After a fruitless search, the vessel left unable to locate the source of the feared drug. Surprisingly, within a few days after the cutter departed, opium trading was back to normal and available for customers in the Chinatown area on Canon Perdido Street.

Marijuana-Moonshine

The smuggling and use of marijuana in the Basin was a problem even in the 1920s. In August of 1924, Ventura County sheriff deputies discovered a large plot of land devoted to growing the outlawed plant in the backyard of a resident of A Street in Oxnard. To hide the tall weed, the person had planted corn around his crop.

The **Star Free Press** reported that a state narcotics agent, known only as Earl, said, "This is the biggest lot of marihuana we have confiscated. We call this a plantation."

The deputies who arrested J. J. Murrietta for growing the plants, estimated its value at $10,000.

On September 1, 1924, the **Santa Barbara Daily News** carried the headline "Mariuana(sic)-Moonshine Maddening Concoction" and reported that two men and a woman were in the county jail because of the use of "the powerful mixture of stimulant...(a) new and terrible concoction... (of) Marahuana-Moonshine." The paper added that the mixture was "being used as knockouts by bootleggers and others who seek to rob men seeking liquor and a spree. Two drops of the concoction is said to be enough to set the ordinary man crazy."

More and more marijuana was being grown in Santa Barbara and the use of the drug was becoming more widespread. The **Daily News** article said, "As the moonshine makers are gradually run out of the county, the marihuana peddler is prospering. He can secrete in his pocket enough of the weed to drive an army into insane acts and he needs but a plot of ground as big as a lettuce patch to keep him supplied."

After Prohibition was repealed in 1933, whiskey smuggling waned, because one could buy it legally. The Volstead Act had its impact on the Basin residents, however. The public had less respect for authority, underground elements had grown wealthy, and many formerly law abiding citizens had been corrupted by the unpopular law.

Fifty years later, in the 1970s, some of the same smuggling rendezvous areas—Smuggler's, Prisoner's, Refugio, Port Hueneme, and Oxnard—became drug transfer centers. The "maddening mariuana concoction" was again being grown illegally in the Basin and posed a serious problem to authorities.

Break Break, Break

Break, break, break,
On thy cold gay stones, O Sea!
And I would that my tongue could utter
The thoughts that arise in me.

B y Alfred Tennyson

Seven

JAPANESE SUBMARINE BRINGS WAR TO CHANNEL

The reality of World War II came to the Santa Barbara Channel three months after the attack on Pearl Harbor when a submarine of the Japanese Imperial Navy shelled the coast of Santa Barbara County. The incident did much to trigger the hysteria that resulted in the relocation and internment of over a hundred thousand coastal Americans of Japanese ancestry.

The event began on February 16, 1942, when an oil company employee at Ellwood Oil Field west of Santa Barbara reported that a 300 foot submarine had come to the surface near the Barnsdall Oil Pier. Calling the tiny Naval Intelligence Office in the Granada Building in Santa Barbara, he told the officer in charge that men had come up out of the hatches and were manning a deck gun.

By the time San Diego naval authorities had been alerted and two patrol planes sent to investigate, the mysterious submarine had submerged and left the scene. During that week, several fishermen reported hearing the sound of diesels at night, which were probably from a submarine on the surface recharging its batteries. Shore observers also reported several sightings that could not be identified by the Navy.

Three days later the sub was sighted again off the Barnsdall Pier. The local Naval Intelligence Officer drove through the Goleta Valley to Ellwood and managed to get a glimpse of the submarine as it was submerging. During this same period local defense capabilities were being reduced by the military. The Coast Guard transferred its Santa Barbara-based patrol boat out of the area, the Marines removed patrol bombers stationed at the Goleta Airport, and the Army withdrew its two howitzers that had been positioned at Ellwood and Coal Oil Point. At 7:00 p.m. on February 23, President Franklin D. Roosevelt started one of his "Fireside Chats" to tell the nation that the country intended to fight the war away from the shores of America. As Americans waited by their radios, the lurking Japanese submarine surfaced again in the Santa Barbara Channel. Later intelligence reports revealed that it was an I-series sub with a length of 348 feet, a 1,950-ton displacement, a 16,000-mile cruising range, and a surface speed of 24 knots. The sub, designated as I-17, carried a crew of 85 officers and men, a reconnaissance plane in a waterproof hangar, a 5.5-inch gun on the afterpart of the deck, and 12 torpedo tubes. She was part of the Japanese Imperial Navy's Sixth Fleet. The Commanding Officer, Captain Kozo Nishino, was familiar with the Santa Barbara Channel. He had sailed Japanese tankers into Ellwood several times before Pearl Harbor to take on crude oil for the Japanese fleet. Nishino's first visit in the late 1930s was an embarrassing one. On the way from the beach to a formal welcoming ceremony, the Japanese Commander fell into a patch of prickly-pear cactus. Humiliated by laughter from oil workers at a nearby well, he supposedly swore to get even.

Captain Nishino did not attempt to hide as he paralleled the coast toward Gaviota on February 23. He reversed and came back to Ellwood in a calm sea and in clear weather. As the undersea vessel approached the Ellwood oil fields, a nine-man gun crew was observed at its deck gun. The ship's speed was reduced at exactly 7:00 p.m., as Americans clustered around their radios to hear FDR's Fireside Chat. The first shots fired by an emeny nation on American soil since 1812 were timed to hit while most Americans were listening to President Roosevelt report on the state of the war.

Seven minutes later, a red flash, followed by a loud explosion from the submarine, shook the windows of Goleta Valley homes. Rushing outdoors, several residents felt terror strike at their hearts as they heard a projectile whistle over their heads. The first shot plowed into one of the slopes of Ellwood Canyon without exploding. Signal Oil Company's superintendent ordered his family and employees into a Southern Pacific Railroad cut as he feared that the Company's gas absorption plant was a target of the marauder.

Ferris W. Borden, Barnsdall Oil's superintendent later reported: "The sub was firing not far from the Bankline Marine loading buoys, which would make the range—one mile off shore . . .A plot of the hits indicate the prime target was the Richfield tank near the highway, but no damage resulted. No retaliatory action taken by either military or civilian personnel at the time of the shelling."

The first shell burst was near the Wheeler's Inn restaurant at Ellwood. Frightened patrons rushed outside to see what was happening. One of the shells made a direct hit on an oil rig. The **Santa Barbara News-Press** reported that the rig was "blasted to bits." Shots burst on the cliffs below the petroleum field, which reached to the water's edge and extended out into the channel. Others arched over the derricks to plow into the ground at the foot of the Santa Ynez Mountains.

Craters from the exploding shells measured over five feet in diameter and several feet deep. Jack Hollister, later a State Senator, who lived up Winchester Canyon about three miles above the oil fields, heard shells whistle over his house and explode in the hills behind it.

The **Santa Barbara News-Press** reported: "With diabolical cunning and boldness the enemy struck as the whole nation was listening to the President's report on the war." Shelling continued for over 30 minutes. Shots whistled over the oil field and exploded on impact in the foothills and surrounding farmlands.

When asked by police for a damage report, the manager of one oil company answered: "I don't know. I'm too busy dodging shells."

The slow and deliberate shelling continued until 7:45 p.m.. A total of about 30 muzzle flashes were observed by a resident at the Trout Club nearby at the San Marcos Pass. Traffic continued to move along the Coast Highway during the shelling.

A local area blackout was ordered at 8:20 p.m., about 20 minutes after the army had shut off all Southern California radio stations so they could not be used as direction-finding beacons by enemy forces. The coast from Santa Maria to Ventura, a distance of almost 100 miles, was soon under blackout restrictions. Within 10 minutes after the warning sirens were sounded, almost all lights along the coastal plain were extinguished.

Santa Barbara's chief of police praised the air raid wardens, Home Guards, and other groups for doing a "swell job." Police officers and Home Guards were sent out from police headquarters to follow up on reported lights from an occasional residence. Air raid wardens took charge of their blocks with what Civilian Defense Coordinator Monroe Rutherford called "promptness and dispatch."

The only problem was the number of automobiles on the streets despite the warning shouts. All traffic was stopped and drivers were ordered to leave their vehicles alongside the road. Even though the headlights of official cars were extinguished as they carried police and Home Guards to their posts, the red stoplights on the rears of the cars flashed in the darkness when drivers applied their footbrakes. This gave rise to numerous reports of mysterious signals being flashed to the enemy. Hundreds of calls were received by authorities asking how people could get home. The answer was always the same: walk.

To a man, Santa Barbara's unit of the California State Guard turned out for duty when news of the attack reached the community. Reporting to the National Guard Armory, soldiers were placed on special defense assignment under regular army orders and dispatched to various locations. Early in the blackout a window in Southwick's Clothing Store was broken by a volunteer guard in order to extinguish lights inside the store.

At the Goleta Airport a group of newspaper reporters and photographers were marooned during the blackout. The army took control and stopped all highway traffic and foot movement at the airport. "Halt, who goes there?" was heard frequently out of the darkness as people moved from their autos toward the airport buildings. Despite the blackout, one red beacon light continued to burn at the airport. Installed on the day of the attack,

80

it remained lighted for several hours during the blackout as engineers looked for the switch that controlled the beacon. Finally, in desperation, the Home Guards shot the light out.

After completing its firing, the submarine headed west and disappeared into a fog bank near Dos Pueblos Ranch. Some two hours later, Army Air Corps planes arrived from Bakersfield. They dropped enough flares over the Channel to make it bright as day, but the Japanese submarine had long since disappeared.

Hundreds of Santa Barbarans walked to beaches to get a better view of the flares being dropped in the sea. The coast was dark except for the moonlight that filtered through a light cloud cover. Lights and arching flares over the ocean added suspense and excitment, making it truly an ironical way to celebrate George Washington's birthday.

It was a real test for civilians, but they handled the crisis calmly. Officials estimated that it took four minutes for most of the lights in the area to be extinguished. Not a single report of panic or looting was received. The police station and the newspaper were swamped with telephone calls reporting flares, flashing lights and suspicious actions.

Along the streets many cars were pulled to the curb, their occupants listening to out-of-state radios report on the total destruction of Santa Barbara. Residents from Santa Maria to Ventura waited in blacked-out houses and listened to the distorted news reports from distant radio stations. Local motion picture theatres remained open as long as patrons wanted to stay. When they ran out of films to show, they arranged talent shows from within the audiences.

Two Los Angeles newspaper men were arrested by city police as they tried to follow a military convoy up the highway. Spotting the unlighted car, the officers took the two reporters into custody and ordered them to appear in police court on a charge of driving without lights.

After the first real test for air raid wardens and the civil defense system in World War II, the all clear was sounded at 12:12 a.m., four hours after the initial alert.

At noon the following day, an Army artillery detachment arrived at Ellwood and set up camp for several days. Military representatives viewed the site of the shelling and found very little damage. Most of the shells were duds and lodged in the foothills behind the oil field. Thirteen years later, during the 1955 Refugio fire, many explosions in the chapparal behind Winchester Canyon were caused by undiscovered duds from the Japanese submarine attack.

The **Santa Barbara News-Press** reported the next day: "An Axis brand of hell was turned loose on the Santa Barbara coastline for the first time last night and the citizenry responded without hysteria."

On the same day as the Ellwood shelling, the German Navy was reported by the press to have sunk the first U.S. warship since America entered the war. The Coast Guard cutter *Alexander Hamilton* was lost through enemy submarine action off the east coast.

Although damage from the shelling was estimated at $500, two days after the attack the following broadcast was monitored from Radio Tokyo:

The U.S. War Department officially announced that Santa Barbara, California, was devastated by enemy bombardment, admitting that a Japanese submarine suddenly appeared on the waters 20 miles west and shelled military establishments in the neighborhood of Ellwood. The United States is not publicizing the damage, however, for fear of the impact on the minds of the public.

The Ellwood attack was only one of two incidents of an enemy vessel firing on American land (the other an equally unsuccessful attack later on Fort Stevens in Oregon), the shelling left a lasting scar on the minds of residents along the Santa Barbara Channel. Blackouts and coast watches were no longer war games, but the real thing for everyone.

EIGHT

SHIPWRECKS AND COLLISIONS
1940 to 1960

As urbanization, industrialization, and population growth increased rapidly after World War II in the Basin, shipping and recreational activities increased in the Channel. More than fifty five ships were destroyed or simply disappeared during the twenty year period from 1940 to 1960. Twenty-two of the sinkings occurred at or near the islands; eight at Anacapa, five each at Santa Cruz and San Nicholas, three at Santa Rosa, and one at Santa Barbara Island. The remaining thirty-three accidents along the coast and in mid channel occurred near Santa Barbara(11), Pt. Conception (4), Pt. Arguello (4), Pt. Dume (3), two each at Carpinteria, Gaviota, Surf and Pt. Sur, and one each at Port Hueneme, Ventura and Pt. Purisima.

Nine known recreational or sport boats sank in the Channel. Among the 46 commercial vessels that were destroyed were 12 fishing boats, two oil drilling support boats, 29 freighters and supply boats, one tanker and one dredge. Nineteen deaths from sea accidents were reported to authorities, down considerably from the 48 deaths in the previous 20-year period.

As use of the Channel piers decreased, commercial shipping accident locations shifted to other places in the Channel. Twelve fishing boats were sunk, eight more than in the previous 20 years. Only one commercial sailing vessel was wrecked, compared to 45 engine propelled vessels, a reflection that the commercial sailing era had ended. The number of strandings or shore wrecked vessels were only 15, down from 27 for the 20-year period, but the number of vessels destroyed by fire increased from four to 13.

Channel Collisions

The number of ships having collisions increased to 10 from four for the previous twenty-year period and included six freighters, two tankers and two sail boats. The sailboats lost in the confrontations. On Oct. 24, 1949, in fog, the oil tanker *Sparrows Point* and the *Max Fisher* collided off Pt. Sur. The *Sparrows Point* caught fire after the collision and burned for hours at sea. Several seamen were injured, but only one was killed. After the fire was finally put out, the *Sparrows Point* was salvaged.

Most collisions occurring in the Channel caused sinkings or serious damage, but in some cases the damaged vessels continued on to their destinations. When the *Coos Bay* (not the old steamer) and the *Stratus* collided in foggy weather eight miles off Anacapa at night on Aug. 22, 1952, a 15 foot hole was torn in the side of the *Coos Bay*. The *Stratus,* not damaged much, continued on to its way. The *Coos Bay* suffered great damage and later sank.

Suomi and *Parramatta* Collide

During a stormy night four miles off Point Arguello, the 49 foot racing yacht, *Suomi,* had a fatal confrontation with the Swedish freighter, *Parramatta.* Although it was raining and visibility was limited, the bridge crew of the *Parramatta* could see Point Arguello's light house four miles away. The big freighter struck the yacht at about 4 a.m. on the morning of April 22, 1955, but hardly felt the blow. But the *Suomi* did.

A crew member of the *Parramatta* reported seeing a faint light off his starboard bow seconds before the ships collided. A Third Mate, Ramon Diaz, Jr., on watch on the port wing of the bridge, did see the light. He went into the wheelhouse and ordered the helmsman "hard to port." Diaz later said that while he neither heard or felt anything, he "had the feeling" that the freighter had hit something. He looked astern to check and saw a white light bobbing on the waves.

The crew of the *Parramatta* reported the incident to the Coast Guard and made a brief search in the stormy darkness. Not finding the boat the freighter continued on. Five men were aboard the *Suomi*. None survived. Only one body was ever recovered. The right leg of the man found had been cut off, presumably by a propeller. The estate of the collision victims later filed suit against the *Parramatta's* owners for $700,000 for the loss of the men and the yacht.

Collision of *Oneida Victory* **and** *W. L. Emmett*

It was a clear night and the Channel was calm. But for some unknown reason, the *Oneida Victory* slashed into the tanker *Emmett's* hull, despite the good visibility. The *Oneida Victory's* bow made a 6-8 ft. gash in the *Emmett* from the deck to below the water line. On the evening of March 2, 1946, Markel Caruthers, a water tender on the *Emmett*, gave his version of the collision. Caruthers said, "I heard the whistle blowing and the next thing I knew this ship came through the side of my room, less than six inches from my head." Caruthers was lucky indeed to be alive to tell the story. Only one man was seriously hurt in the accident. Both ships were wrecked near Pt. Conception as a result of the collision.

Freighters Aground

Several freighters ran aground from 1940 to 1960, but the crews of the stranded ships were rescued in most cases. When the wheat-carrying *Ioannis G. Kulukundis*, a World War II liberty ship went aground on a sandbar in fog near Surf on July 11, 1949, its entire crew of 30 were rescued. Fifteen crew members were also removed safely from the *S.S. Steel Chemist* when it ran aground off San Nicholas Island April 12, 1949. Another liberty ship, the *Patria*, ran aground at Skunk Point, the east end of Santa Rosa Island, on June 21, 1954. The Greek crew of 40 was rescued successfully. The ship was abandoned, but later refloated and salvaged.

Nancy B **Goes Under**

What began as a pleasant fishing trip on their converted cabin cruiser, resulted in the death of Bernice Brown's husband (Roy) and brother-in-law(John) and her harrowing experience with the unbelievably harsh winds and seas of the Channel. The Browns had fished on the *Nancy B* for three years and knew its characteristics. Unfortunately, they did not know the Channel's sometimes unpleasant nature. The trio left Santa Monica at midnight in March 1946 for Santa Cruz Island. At 9:30 in the morning the boat was about half way between Anacapa and Santa Cruz Island in rough seas. Mrs. Brown vividly describes what happened next:

The wind seemed to come at us from all directions. I hate to say how tall the waves were because I don't think anybody would believe me-they were 50 feet high, I thought.

Suddenly we took a sea over the stern and it flooded our motor. My husband opened the hatch to see what he could do and at that moment another wave came inboard and **Nancy B.** *was swamped.*

Roy turned and said: "Honey, it'll have to be the skiff."

John said: "She won't live two minutes in this sea."

Roy said: "I said—the skiff!"

We all got in the small boat and started away from the **Nancy B.** *We got about 40 feet away and it seemed to me like a whole sea poured into the skiff. She turned over and the next thing I knew I was in the water.*

I thought I had better swim to the **Nancy B.** *I reached her side and held on but the seas were so strong that I couldn't board her.*

When I looked back at the skiff I saw Roy and John hanging on and then Roy started swimming toward me. He got about half way then he went down. The last I saw of him was his arm thrust out of a wave top.

I never did see what happened to John. I was alone.

Frightened but not panicking, Bernice Brown stayed near the boat for about a half hour. Using an empty gasoline can as a support, she swam for about seven miles to the rocky, unfriendly exterior of Anacapa Island. She climbed onto some rocks and held on for her life.

Brown spent the night clinging to her rocky perch. In the morning she swam for about four hours along the cliffs until she saw four cabins above her. With great effort she climbed up the steep bank until she reached the deserted buildings. Ripping off a boarded door Brown found food and water inside. For two weeks she lived in the cabin, going outside every day to gather wood and keep a fire burning to attract attention to her existence. After being shipwrecked on Anacapa for 14 days, a Coast Guard boat saw her fire and rescued her.

Trying to eat a pleasant dinner prepared by her rescuers, Brown found she could not down it or eat much for several days later. Reflecting on the terrible ordeal Brown said, "I feel better but not about fishing and about the ocean. I never want to see it again."

Sea Bee

A year later in October of 1947, the sardine fishing boat, *Sea Bee*, encountered large swells off Santa Barbara and paid a high price for its crew's carelessness. A deck hatch left open allowed sea water from the huge waves to pour below causing the $35,000 boat to swamp and sink in ten minutes. One man drowned and seven were rescued in the accident.

Sebastian L.

A strange event caused the sinking of the fifty foot fishing boat, *Sebastian L.* While fishing about 35 miles south by south west of Point Sur, an anchor became loose in rough seas. The anchor commenced to punch a hole in the hull of the boat before it was discovered, too late. The ship sank quickly. The three men onboard were lucky to be rescued so far out to sea.

The *Bob and Jocko*

The fishing boat *Bob and Jocko* mysteriously disappeared on April 28, 1949. Two men onboard at the time were never found. A third man would undoubtedly be dead also if he had not sensed some impending catastrophe. Bob Miller was onboard the *Bob and Jocko* as it headed out of Santa Barbara harbor for a day of fishing in the Channel. The other two men, now missing, became involved in a furious argument. The seriousness of the altercation so alarmed Miller that he demanded the two men turn the boat around and put him ashore. Miller's premonition of trouble and assertiveness saved his life.

Five years later on May 5, 1954, divers found the *Bob and Jocko* in deep water off the east end of Santa Cruz Island. No trace of the two missing men was found. No one knows why the *Bob and Jocko* sank.

The *Trade Winds* before its tragedy in October 1967.
(Star-Free Press)

NINE

NEW HARBORS AND MORE ACCIDENTS
THE 1960s

With the construction of two new recreational and commercial fishing harbors in Ventura County during the 1960s, fishing and recreational boating activity in the Channel and around the islands greatly increased, and the number of accidents and water oriented deaths and injuries also grew. Several devastating storms swept through the Channel Basin during the 1960s, sinking many boats and damaging shore facilities and hundreds of other vessels. From 1960 to 1970 more than 90 boating accidents occurred in which 84 boats were destroyed and at least 48 people were killed.

A total of 81 people died from boating (48), diving (5), swimming (17), and aircraft and helicopter (11) accidents. Thirty-one of the 90 boats sank, 48 capsized, ran aground, caught fire or were destroyed, and five collided with a boat or an object.

Shipwreck and Boating Accidents

Oil Exploration Ship Accidents

As the oil companies stepped up their exploration activity in the moody Channel to produce oil, accidents began to happen to their fleet of boats. On May 8, 1960, the 96-foot-long oil exploration boat *Brant* caught fire while off El Capitan. Fearing the boat would explode the crew of eight abandoned the ship hurriedly, jumping into the water. As if angry at its bad treatment, the *Brant* continued to run under power, with no one at the helm, in circles for several miles until it finally sank. The eight men were rescued and were lucky not to have been run over by the burning boat.

Tanker and Freighters

The 5000 ton Greek tanker/freighter, *S.S. Ellin,* ran aground in foggy weather north of Point Arguello on Dec. 16, 1963. Five years later on June 16, 1968, the *Cossatot*, a 523 ft. long tanker, loaded with 5,000,000 gallons of jet fuel, hit the 492 ft. long freighter, the *Copper State*, in midchannel. The two ships, both going at a good clip, hit bow to bow. The blow from the confrontation disabled the *Cossatot,* which had to be towed to San Pedro. The *Copper State* was left with a 20 ft. breach in its bow and a huge gash below the water line but was able to make port under its own power. Luckily no crewman were injured, no fire occurred, and no jet fuel was spilled into the Channel.

Triple Crown **Tragedy**

The worst oil boat tragedy in the 1960s was the sudden sinking of the 174 ft. offshore oil service vessel *Triple Crown.* The ship left Port Hueneme on Saturday, Nov. 24, 1968 to assist in relocating the drilling barge *Blue Water II* belonging to the Humble Oil Co. The sea was calm and smooth when the one million dollar ship entered the Channel. The *Crown* was considered the latest design in anchor-handling supply boats at the time. This assignment was its second in the Channel.

Shortly after three a.m. on November 25, in rough seas and with a 35 knot wind blowing, the *Triple Crown* started to list. The crewmen had just completed hauling in the eighth and last anchor off the drilling platform. About 800 tons of anchors and chain were on board. When the boat started to list the captain, George Gaskill, 34, reported: "There was only a few moments' indication that trouble was brewing. I sent a man down to wake up any sleeping crewmen then all of a sudden the vessel went down stern first and we were all in the cold water."

Crewman Kindt asleep below reported that someone came into the crew quarters and yelled, "'Wake up!' And I got out."

The surviving crewmen said that the stern went down first as if it was being pulled down by chains snagged on some underwater cable or object. The sinking happened about four miles offshore and eight miles southwest of Santa Barbara Harbor at around 3:45 a.m. in 300 ft. of water. Of the 25 crewmen, 16 dove off the boat and hung on to floating debris. Nine men were missing. After about thirty minutes the tugboat *Pacific Saturn* rescued the cold men from the 52 degree water.

Later divers went below to search for the missing men and determine the cause of the accident. Seven bodies were found trapped in the sunken boat. One diver said the deck was rippled crosswise, generally buckled and "doesn't seem to be intact." Commenting on how such a big ship could have its plates and deck buckled, commercial diver Laddie Handelman said, "Nothing surprises me in this ocean." Two other crewmen were missing and presumed dead.

Over 2000 pages of testimony was taken at a nine-day Coast Guard inquiry. It was determined that the sinking probably occurred because a deck hatch was blocked open by an anchor permiting water from the breaking waves to run below. An engine failure also contributed to the accident. Even the latest and safest oil support ship of its type had met defeat in the tempestuous Santa Barbara Channel.

Fishing Boat Accidents

At least 15 fishing boats had serious accidents in the 1960s: seven sank, six ran aground, one was in a collision and one almost sank from hull damage. Of the 15, 10 were commercial and five were recreational or sport boats. Some of the fishing boats were involved in strange events and unexplained happenings. The Point Conception area, as usual, claimed a heavy quota of boats. The 34 ft. *Vega* went aground there in high winds as did the 50 ft. *Glennis C.* and the abalone boat *El Fungo*. Two other smaller fishing boats also went aground north of Point Arguello.

Little K

On Dec. 6, 1965, the 28 ft. fishing boat *Little K* was found beached on Santa Cruz Island. The boats running lights were on and the automatic pilot was operating. A small poodle dog was alive on the boat but the owner, Frank Matz, was missing. The hull had a small hole in it. A search was made for Matz, but he was not found. Authorities surmised that Matz had motored to the island at night and hit the shore. But why was he gone? What had really happened? The poodle was a mute witness to the event that caused the accident. The dog was returned to Mrs. Matz and the cabin cruiser towed back to the mainland.

Sea Duce

The abalone boat, *Sea Duce*, moving fast under power failed to notice the guy wires holding an oil barge. The impact of the collision with the guy wires sheared off the *Sea Duce's* flying bridge and controls and disabled the boat.

Ventura

While about two miles off Channel Islands Harbor, the 44 ft. bait boat, *Ventura*, encountered some large swells and swamped. The two men on board jumped overboard to save themselves as the boat sank in water about 35 ft. deep. The men were in the water about two and half hours before being rescued.

Not having any insurance, the owners attempted to raise the boat. Divers attached empty drums to the boat and filled them with air. The *Ventura* made an ascent to the surface, but four of the drums broke loose exploding into the air. The boat plunged once again to the bottom stern first. Not willing to give up, the owners next secured a line to the *Ventura* and towed it, under water, into Channel Islands Harbor for another salvage attempt in more shallow water. The cause of the sinking was not determined.

Kitrie

The *Kitrie,* a 40 ft. fishing boat, disappeared March 18, 1967 in the Channel. Later one body and some boat debris were found 11 miles off Point Dume. The body of the second crewman was never found. Two years later on June 29, 1969, the *Kitrie* was accidently found by fisherman diving for a lost net. The boat went down nearly four miles off Channel Island Harbor.

Small Boat Accidents

Out of the 89 boats destroyed or severely damaged, 27 of them were small boats of 23 ft. or less. Most of them were motor boats with an outboard engine. Of the 27 small boats in accidents,

11 sank and 16 were destroyed in some other manner. Ten people died in the accidents and over 50 people were rescued. The suvivors of many of the small boat sinkings and groundings suffered some harrowing experiences.

A trio, including two men and a nephew, unwisely motored out to Anacapa Island from the Ventura Harbor in a 13 ft. open motor boat on a clear, calm day on March 23, 1966. Typically, the wind came up and the waves increased in height. Finding the distance back to the mainland too far, the trio decided to make for Anacapa and possible safety.

Near the island the waves became more choppy and dangerous. The boat was thrust over a reef by the force of a wave and tossed 20 to 30 ft. into the air and dropped with a crash into the surf. The blow ripped the bottom out of the small boat and the surf destroyed the rest of the boat quickly, the men claimed.

The boaters made it to the beach, but faced climbing a 250-foot-high cliff to escape the pounding surf and rising tide. Anacapa lighthouse was their goal, but it was not possible to reach it. A compromise was forced on them because of the sheerness of the cliff. The three climbed to the highest part of the beach, built a fire and shivered through the night. The next day around 2:00 p.m. a naval craft from Port Hueneme spotted them.

The trio was lucky, despite their unpleasant experience. A 13 ft. open boat is too small for trips to the Islands. The four passengers of a 17 ft. outboard cabin cruiser suffered a worse fate on May 2, 1964, when it was overturned by waves near Anacapa and four people, including a father and his son, were drowned.

One 16 ft. cabin cruiser capsized in stormy weather on Hollywood Beach in such a manner that one of the passengers, a 43 year old man, was trapped in the overturned boat for thirty minutes. After his rescue he said, "It was awful, I just knew I was dead." One person was killed in the grounding and another rescued. The boat had been given assistance earlier in the Channel when it had run out of gas in midchannel at night.

Large Power Boat Accidents

Small boats were not the only vessels destroyed by the sea and the mistakes of skippers. Large motor vessels sank and ran aground in increasing numbers. Of the total of 89 vessels destroyed, 66 were power boats, of which 39 were 25 ft. or longer.

Trade Winds Tragedy

In October of 1967, a party of 25 happy guests aboard the expensive 55 ft. motor yacht, *Trade Winds*, motored out of the Ventura Harbor about 9:00 p.m. bound for Channel Island Harbor for a celebration dinner. They never made it. The group on board was having cocktails on the clear night and enjoying the cruise as guests of Merrill Shapiro. The boat motored along the coast parallel and close to the shore. Near the mouth of the Santa Clara River, where the water tends to be shallow, two of the passengers noticed the waves getting larger. The fathometer was operating, but no one was checking it. The boat's speed was over 10 knots.

As reported in the **Star-Free Press**, guest Ray Culp told Shipiro, "I think we're too close to shore." Another passenger, Al Young, yelled at Shapiro, at the helm, "Turn out to sea." But Shapiro turned back in toward shore. "He apparently became confused or misread his compass," guest Jack Jamar reported. Suddenly a huge wave hit the yacht forcing it over on its side with a tremendous crash and spray of water. The boat was only about 100 to 150 yards off shore at the time. Shapiro thought he was a half mile out to sea.

Shapiro said he looked seaward at the warning and "it was just like an avalanche—like a tidal wave. The next thing I knew I was on the floor with a broken leg." The force of the huge wave knocked 12 of the unsuspectinng passengers into the raging surf. Most of the guests were not wearing life preservers. The evening of fun changed instantaneously to a nightmare of panic and chaos. A second big wave smashed the *Trade Winds* onto her side a second time washing the remaining passengers into the surf, except for Jamar and Shapiro.

Shapiro related later; "I thought everyone was gone. I tried to get up to the wheel, but I couldn't move." Thinking clearly, Jack Jamar took over the boat's wheel and manuvered the big cruiser out of the surf without hitting any of the people in the water. Mrs. Jamar said, "He kept the boat away from the people, so the passengers in the water would not be injured."

Without Jamar's quick reaction and good seamanship, undoubtedly more people would have been run over or hit by the propeller, or the boat would have capsized on top of them. Jamar notified authorities of the accident as he took the boat back to Ventura Harbor.

Two women and one man died in the tragedy. It is amazing that more were not killed. Rescue personnel rushed to the beach and helped the injured and half drowned people ashore and into cars and ambulances. Later at the Ventura County General Hospital emergency room, a teenage daughter of Sam Gillard waited anxiously for news of him. Her girl friend kept her company. Except for two passengers who had been hospitalized, all other victims had left. Mrs. Gillard, still wet from her forced dunking and dazed from the ordeal, sat on a couch near her daughter. The Deputy Coroner, Leo Richardson, approached Mrs. Gillard and the two girls at about midnight and sadly told them that Mr. Gillard had been found dead. Their hopes for Gillard's rescue were over.

At a Coast Guard board of inquiry later, it was determined that Shapiro had been negligent and charges were filed against him for bringing the yacht too close to shore--causing the tragedy. The Coast Guard report found that eight to 10 ft. waves had come over the stern and that the bow had hit bottom knocking the passengers to the boat's deck. Incoming waves then washed them into the sea. Shapiro was fined $1,000 by the Coast Guard.

Sailboat Accidents

A total of 19 sailboats sank, capsized, ran aground or were destroyed. The *Patience,* a 52 ft. boat was found aground near Point Conception with no one on board. Two men died when the *Kitty* sank off the Mesa. Several catamarans capsized in the Channel. Two men were lost off Santa Barbara when their catamaran overturned. The one survivor was in the water 12 hours before his rescue. Three men were in the water near Point Mugu for 48 hours when their 18 ft. sloop overturned.

Marjorie K

Only two miles from Pelican Bay, at Santa Cruz Island, a spark ignited gasoline on the sloop *Marjorie K*. The Santa Barbara couple on board realized the danger and tossed their rubber dinghy and themselves overboard. A few moments later the gas tank blew up ripping away part of the deck and cabin of the 26 ft. long boat. The *Marjorie K* sank quickly. The couple was adrift in the small life raft for 16 hours in 15 ft. high waves before being spotted by some passing fisherman. They were taken to Smugglers Cove and to Walter Hoffman's 55 ft. motor boat—glad to be alive.

Strange and Unusual Accidents

Marie Disappears

One of the strangest boating accidents of the 1960s was the disappearance of the *Marie*, a converted 42 foot World War II landing craft (LCVP). The Raytheon Company had chartered the boat to conduct secret scientific studies. Seven men were on board when the *Marie* headed for Santa Cruz Island on June 11, 1960. The ship vanished without a call of distress or a signal for help. When notified the ship was missing, the Coast Guard searched the Channel for about 39 hours, but to no avail.

How could a group of experienced people in a well conditioned ship disappear? Nine years later in November 1969, an abalone diver discovered the *Marie* by accident in 55 ft. of water about two and a half miles off Santa Cruz Island. Divers could not determine the cause of the sinking and indicated it was not practical to raise the boat. No trace of the seven men was found.

Cement Truck Plunges To The Bottom

In September of 1966, a barge was employed to haul a big cement truck to Santa Cruz Island to do some work. At the start of the voyage the driver was apparently told that in order to draw full pay or be elgible for certain benefits he had to remain in the truck's cab. Compliance with the rules cost the driver his life.

About three miles out to sea, the wind came up and the sea became rough. Foundering in several large swells the barge turned over and dumped the huge cement truck, with the driver still in the cab, into 300 ft. of water. The barge's two crew members escaped, but the truck driver was never found.

A Surprise Launching Opens Ventura Harbor

When the Ventura Harbor was completed and opened in 1963 for boat usage, officials had a surprise first launching. The first vessel launched floated out to the middle of the harbor and slowly sank. The vessel was not a vessel at all, but a Ford Falcon. The car, parked beside the harbor, apparently wanted to try the waters and rolled down the bank into the water. Later the car was pulled out of the harbor and returned to its owner. The bank launching point has been known as Falcon Point ever since.

The Little Amphibious Car That Couldn't

Even stranger vessels ventured into the Channel. An amphibious car was victimized in 1966. Seeing how calm the sea was on the morning of December 21, three youths took their amphibious car into the Channel to fish. In the afternoon the winds came up and the waves became higher. The trio headed back to the Ventura Harbor, but it was too late. Waves of 12 to 15 ft. were breaking at the entrance.

As the amphibious car approached the surging entrance, fishermen and other people on the jetty yelled warnings to the trio. The car was no match for the foaming, pounding waves and was soon out of control. The car headed for the rocks stern first. People on shore shouted for the group to jump and swim for shore. The warnings were heeded this time, they jumped. The car slammed against the rocks again and again. In a few minutes it was reduced to junk. One of the youths said later that it was his first and last voyage in an amphibious car.

Aircraft and Helicopter Crashes

Four aircraft and helicopter crashes resulted in 11 deaths during the 1960s. Two oil company helicopters, serving offshore platforms, mysteriously crashed in the same area under clear and mild weather conditions. The first helicopter disappeared while returning to Carpinteria from a platform in November of 1966. No radio communication was received from the pilot indicating engine or weather difficulties. No survivors, wreckage, or debris was ever found. A search was initiated for the craft as soon as the company realized it had not returned to its destination. The pilot and three passengers aboard were killed in the crash.

The second helicopter, flying employees of the Western Off-shore Drilling and Exploration Co., went down in April of 1968 about nine miles from Carpinteria. The copter had picked up four men from the drilling barge *WODECO* and was returning them to their shore facility. As happened in the earlier accident, the visibility was excellent, almost 25 miles, and the helicopter was operating well. The pilot sent no distress signal or any warning of trouble.

When the oil company realized the copter was overdue, the Coast Guard was notified and a search begun. The Coast Guard spotted debris, including the log book and the craft's pontoons, eight miles off the coast. The helicopter owners, Utility Helicopter, who had never had a fatality in the seven years it had been flying in the Channel, were mystified at the cause of the accident. The helicopter had adequate fuel, no mechanical problems and was flying at noontime with good visibility.

Diving and Swimming Accidents

As the Basin's population grew and boaters made more trips to the islands, the number of diving and swimming accidents multiplied. Five scuba divers were killed and seventeen swimmers drowned during the 60s in the Channel. Some of the diving deaths were very strange. One island diver speared a large fish that immediately dove downward to escape. Unforunately, Rothstein, the diver, had attached the line to his body and was not prepared for the sudden diving action of the fish into deep water. Realizing his danger, the diver pulled out his knife and cut the the line. Unfortunately, it was too late. He had been pulled underwater too long and too deeply to survive. His body was found on the bottom in 45 ft. of water. The fish had taken the spear and the cut line and disappeared.

Damage From Winds and Storms

Several devastating storms swept through the Channel Basin during the 1960s that caused the sinking of many boats and damaged shore facilities and vessels. On January 16, 1966, par-ticulary high winds made their damaging presence known in the

Basin. Onshore thousands of homes went without electricity due to falling trees knocking out power lines.

Pleasure boats visiting the islands were caught in dangerous situations. Many boaters were stranded for days on the islands. Several boats were sunk by winds reaching over 60 knots.

At sea, the 26 ft. yawl, *Eros*, lost its mast and sank due to the fierce winds. The 31 ft. power boat, *Brandie*, sank. The *Trilogy* and other recreational boats were smashed against the island's rocky shore by the northeast wind. Over 30 boaters were rescued.

Caught in the winds at Scorpion Cove on Santa Cruz Island, Don Walters, an experienced skipper, claimed the Channel winds were the worst he had ever seen. Walters said, "The winds came up about 8 p.m. and we decided to get out of there." Walter's wife Mary said, "We had trouble getting the anchor up and finally bent it and broke the chain roller getting it up. Swells were about 10 ft. and wind was blowing about 60 knots." It took the Walters in their beautiful Kettenburg sail boat, *King Don*, seven and a half hours to make the 18 miles back to Channel Islands Harbor.

The winds blew a surfer a half mile out to sea before he could be rescued. The 65 ft., *Island Queen*, a sport fishing boat, barely made it back to Port Hueneme. The waves had cracked its hull letting water into the cabin. It was a good day to stay home.

Channel Storms Destroy Ventura Harbor

January and February of 1969 were an ugly time in the Channel. Shortly before the Union Oil Company's well blew up in the Channel on January 28, pouring oil into the basin, a storm, reaching its peak on January 25, released over nine inches of rainfall in a few days. It was the heaviest rainfall since 1943. In Ventura County, the downpour could not be contained within the Santa Clara River levees built to protect the adjacent land. The river made a breach in the levee near the mouth and, seeking an easy route to the sea, cut across Harbor Boulevard into the Ventura Harbor. Several docks and boats were lost or damaged. The Ventura sanitation plant, next to the harbor, was flooded, damaged, and forced to shut down.

Thousands of acres of land were flooded near the Santa Clara River clogging streets and damaging houses, farm land, and commercial property. The damage was estimated to be about

$250,000 for the harbor and $100,000 for the sewer plant. Little did the public know that the January storm was only the preliminary event. A few weeks later the major storm hit.

It started raining in February 1969 and continued nonstop for nine consecutive days. The Santa Clara River reached its saturation point once again and broke through its banks to really flood the Ventura Harbor. Unfortunately, the harbor had been built in the river's original flood plain. The river needed elbow room and was not intimidated by any manmade structure like a boat harbor.

The river ripped through the harbor on February 25, at 2:30 a.m., sinking, taking out to sea, or destroying about 100 of the 295 boats in the harbor at the time. Docks, mooring and several banks forming the harbor were wiped out.

Adjacent to the harbor, Union Oil Company's $100,000 bulk plant was destroyed. Six of the company's oil storage tanks were also demolished. Three of the tanks were carried out to sea by the raging river. From the tanks an additional 120,000 gallons of oil spilled into the already oily channel trying to recover from the Union Oil's platform "A" blow out of January 28th.

As the river swept through the harbor, boats were destroyed by crashing against each other, smashing into telephone poles, trees, oil drums, docks, and a variety of other debris. Some boats, their dock tethers snapped loose, floated majestically out to the harbor entrance where the graceful ships were pounded to pieces by the turbulent meeting of the river and the sea's huge breakers. It was a sad sight. Many boat owners failing to reach their boats, watched in agony at the sight of their craft being destroyed. Fortunately, some boats were miraculously saved.

The 48 ft. racing cutter, *Freedom,* was on its way to the entrance slaughter house, but was "caught" in time by some sailors. Other rescue attempts endangered the lives of the sailors. One group, attempting to save a large power cruiser, became stranded on the boat and was being carried rapidly out to possible death at the entrance of the harbor. Luckily, a fishing boat crew pulled the group off in time to avert disaster.

The wreckage and devastation at the harbor was both horrendous and fascinating. The destruction of the harbor seemed to be the last straw in its already troubled history. The Ventura Port

District had a record of previous difficulties trying to finance the construction of the harbor, solve the entrance silting, and other difficult physical and legal problems. Community voices were heard demanding that the harbor be abandoned, the entrance closed, and the basin be made into a lake and houses built around the perimeter.

The damage was extensive. Over 900,000 cubic yards of silt were deposited in the harbor basin. Utilities were torn out. The 540 boat slips destroyed were valued at more than one-half million dollars. Harbor business and commecial fishing were paralyzed. The total cost of the damage was estimated to be over $4,000,000.

Ventura Harbor entrance during flood, February 1969.

Ventura Harbor Rebuilding Begins

Interest slowly evolved to rebuild. Boaters, city officials, Chamber of Commerce and Harbor District personnel mustered support and started making progress in refinancing and rebuilding the harbor. Legal problems with disgruntled boaters and harbor contractors continued, however. After the storm, 163 Ventura boat owners joined together in a $2,650,000 suit against the Port District, claiming that the District had been negligent in not warning them of the possible danger from the storm. The case was finally settled out of court six years later for only $127,000.

TEN

CONTEMPORARY SMUGGLERS
AND PIRATES

Demand for drugs in the Basin and the Los Angeles region generated a fleet of smugglers in the Channel during the seventies and eighties. Prior to 1974, federal agencies had few indicators that marine smuggling was occurring in the Santa Barbara Channel. Most marine smuggling was thought to occur around San Diego. Many small boats brought drugs from Mexico to Shelter Island and other landing points near San Diego. Finding that drug smugglers were operating greater distances and in larger boats, the U.S. Customs Service opened an office in Ventura County in 1977 to better monitor and survey smuggling operations. Every year, as the police become more efficient in identifying and nabbing violators, the smugglers become more sophisticated and clever at avoiding capture.

Black Weber Group

A sophisticated group of former Navy SEALS, similar to the Army's "Green Berets," and a few other men formed the *Black Weber* Group in San Diego. Operating a drug-smuggling operation first in San Diego, they later expanded to the Santa Barbara Channel area. To get needed underwater equipment for their operation, the *Black Weber* Group arranged to "lose" Navy equipment while involved in underwater diving and training missions. The group returned later to pick up the equipment.

To fulfill their need for a headquarters in the Basin area, they rented a house owned by the State of California at Malibu. The group used small boats to bring drugs ashore, including a 30-foot Sea Ray. Joseph R. Willey of the U.S. Custom's service in the Basin says smugglers who bring in drugs worth several million dollars think nothing of sinking or abandoning small boats when it is convenient to their operation.

After months of surveillance of the *Weber* Group, the Customs Service and other law authorities indicted them in 1977. Some members were arrested late in 1981 in Santa Barbara. The group's assets, estimated at over $7 million, were seized by federal authorities. Another $2 million was seized later.

Harmon Rabreau Group

The *Harmon Rabreau* Group was involved in smuggling from San Diego to Washington State. They had an association with drug dealers on the East Coast. This group used fishing boats as decoys to hide their Pacific Coast operation before being indicted in 1978.

Red Baron Case

On a Saturday afternoon, January 17, 1976, after a long sea chase, the 60-foot *Red Baron* fishing boat was seized by authorities eight miles from Channel Islands Harbor. The *Baron* had been followed by State Fish and Game, Channel Islands Harbor Patrol boats, and a Ventura County Sheriff's helicopter. On board was found more than nine tons of marijuana estimated to be worth $800,000 or several million on the retail market. A total of 13 people were arrested in the case. The marijuana was wrapped in bricks weighing 2.2 pounds.

The *Baron* was a "mother ship" bringing marijuana from Mexico and unloading the cargo into a fleet of smaller boats 100 to 150 miles offshore or near the Islands. The smaller boats then took the goods to shore where it was unloaded. This group had a house adjacent to the Channel Islands Harbor, across the street from another house owned by the *Black/Weber* smuggling group.

The *Red Baron* group had several trailerable boats, 28-foot skipjacks that were pulled out of the water onshore at harbors and towed to an industrial park warehouse on Palma Drive in

Ventura. Their building was near the California Highway Patrol Office. The marijuana was distributed to their network from the warehouse. Customs Officers followed the smugglers to their warehouse before arresting them. In addition to the nine tons of marijuana, officials seized the 60-foot trawler, one 29-foot Aquacraft cabin cruiser, a racing boat, two 20-foot skipjacks, two trucks, and a Porsche. Customs Officers and local police started surveillance of the *Red Baron* Gang in 1975 and arrested them in January, 1976.

At the end of the smugglers' trial, United States Federal Judge Manuel Real ruled that the seized marijuana was not admissible evidence. The Judge claimed the marijuana was improperly taken by officers as they did not have "founded suspicion" to contact two of the smuggling suspects and ask to search their boat and truck, even though several tons of marijuana were found. The federal, state and local agency personnel who had worked hard to capture the smugglers were bitterly disappointed.

The case was appealed, but finally won by the government on the basis that the smuggling suspects had been investigated and followed for several months preceding their arrests and that Federal Custom Officers had a legal and legitimate right to be involved in the case. The entire legal process took several years to complete and was costly to the taxpayers.

Using legal appeals and continuances, defense lawyers for the 13 arrested smugglers managed to stave off the suspects' ultimate conviction until 1980, five years later. After their hard work on the case, Joseph Willey said Customs officials were not happy with the light sentences ultimately given the offenders.

No-Name Sailboat Case

Santa Cruz Island was the scene of another smuggling boat seizure on June 14, 1976. U.S. Customs Officers and Coast Guard officials boarded a 51-foot ketch near Santa Cruz Island and arrested four men. Two tons of marijuana were found on the sailboat. Two of the suspects seized had been arrested five months earlier in the *Red Baron* case. While out on bail, the *Baron* men continued their chosen line of work.

The arrests were made because a patrolling Coast Guard boat became suspicious of the erratic and sloppy manner in which the sailboat was being handled. Also, the vessel was without a name or registration number. A couple of sailing lessons might have saved their skins, at least for a while. While the sailboat was allegedly stolen, the owner was suspected of being part of the caper.

Officials reported that the ketch had picked up the marijuana from a "mother ship" near San Clemente Island, 50 miles south of Catalina Island. Before the case came to trial, one of the accused was found dead of a heroin overdose. A Customs Officer said it was a suspicious death, as the man had never been known to use heroin. The offenders were given five-year sentences after their conviction.

Siboney Boat Case

After an investigation of over a month, with the help of the Santa Barbara Sheriff's Department, the U.S. Customs Office seized the 45-foot powerboat *Siboney* off Santa Cruz Island. The "leased" boat from Anchorage, Alaska, was a mother ship and had four people on board. Three and one-half tons of marijuana were seized and ten people arrested. Two Santa Barbara County Sheriff's undercover agents were approached by members of the land-based off-loading crew at one point in the investigation and found themselves in a dangerous situation. Faced with some sharp questioning, the agents became aggressive and threatened to blow up the boat if they were not cut into the smuggling operation. The ruse worked, but the agents were more than a little nervous about the danger to their lives.

Smugglers' Mode of Operation

As the Customs Service, Drug Enforcement Department, U.S. Coast Guard, FBI, and local police agencies have increased their surveillance of marine smugglers, drug smugglers have changed their mode of operation and level of sophistication. The present style is to have large mother ships, 100 to 200 feet long, sail along the Pacific Coast and unload a portion of the cargo into smaller boats for distribution to different communities along their route. Airplanes are used also in the Channel. Planes drop their cargo in waterproof containers at designated places at sea to be fished out later by boats.

Many ships, upon being discovered, scuttle their craft with the evidence. In July of 1981, the *Polaris,* 128 feet long, was scuttled by its crew when a Coast Guard cutter approached it. A similar event occurred in 1980 when a Coast Guard C-130 flew over the *Gladstone,* over 100 feet in length, a suspected mother ship. The crew opened the sea cocks and sank the ship rather than take a chance on being boarded.

East Coast Crackdown Affects Basin

With concern over drug use growing, federal, state, and local law enforcement agencies have been cooperating more in recent years. In 1979, 169 maritime seizures occurred nationwide; in 1980, 304; and in 1981, 402, most of which were on the East Coast. Authorities on the East Coast, in particular, have become much tougher on drug dealers. Harsh sentences are now being given to convicted drug smugglers and dealers.

Because the East Coast is closer to the supply source, in Colombia and Central America, greater drug traffic occurs there. Recently, with Coast Guard assistance, five "choke points" have been blockaded at sea off the East Coast, making smuggling more hazardous than in the past. As a result, smugglers have shifted more of their marine operations to the West Coast.

Undercover drug agents have difficulty infiltrating drug smugglers operations because they are so close knit, usually formed by people who have been associates for years. The relationships typically begin in the military, at work, or in high school. Drug-dealing groups in the Basin have formed from abalone divers, roofers, and military men. A group of abalone divers who made as much as $40,000 a year each from legitimate diving went into drug smuggling in the Basin when the market for abalone was down. In most cases drug dealers are good friends and trust each other. Anyone trying to befriend and join their group is under instant suspicion.

The Santa Barbara Channel is a prime target for drug smugglers because of the many hiding places available along the four islands and the coast and its nearness to the huge Los Angeles and southern California market. The Pacific Coast does not have natural "choke points" as does the East Coast, making it harder to monitor marine traffic. Ships with a goal of illicit trade can approach the California coast from hundreds of different directions from the sea, making surveillance difficult.

Present smugglers operate in ways amazingly similar to the smugglers of the Spanish California days, and the prohibition days of the 1920s and early 30s. Customs Officers suspect that Smuggler's Cove, or the east coast of Santa Cruz, the east coast of Santa Rosa, Point Dume, Pitas Point (Ventura County), the coast off of Port Hueneme, Ventura, and west of Gaviota may be smuggling areas. A look at a chart of the Channel illustrates that Smuggler's Cove at the east end of Santa Cruz gives a smuggler an excellent location to make a run to the coast of Santa Barbara or Ventura counties.

Drug-carrying boats have been seized off Point Dume, Ventura, and Gaviota. On Halloween of 1976, the 70-foot *Dong Phat* was seized and discovered to be carrying six tons of narcotic thai sticks. Sixteen people were arrested. During 1976, 18 boats were seized in the Channel for smuggling and narcotic violations. One, the 40-foot *Big Daddy*, had been stolen from the Ventura Harbor. After 1976, the marine seizures in the Channel declined. In 1977, two airplanes, but no boats were seized. One vessel was seized in 1978, two vessels in 1979, and none in 1980. Activity picked up again in the 1980s, however.

Conflict With Contemporary Pirates in Channel

During the prohibition period, the losers, in conflicts between bootleggers were often dumped in the Mojave desert or the Pacific Ocean. The Channel undoubtedly had its share of bodies dumped during prohibition as it has during the contemporary drug smuggling period. Local newspapers often report the discovery of an unidentified body or a skeleton picked clean by fish and crabs. During the 1970s, several piracy cases in the Channel were uncovered.

Piracy and Murder of Robert Finkbine at Sea

Robert Finkbine, 45, owned a 45 ft. sailboat and kept it in Marina del Rey near Los Angeles. On October 13, 1973, Finkbine's boat was taken out of the marina. Finkbine told no one that he was leaving. A few days later on October 18th, Finkbine's sister noticed the boat was missing and notified authorities. A sea search was made but neither Finkbine nor his sailboat could be found.

Suspecting foul play, Los Angeles County Sheriff detectives began a search of the recreational harbors along the coast. With the help of the Ventura County Sheriff's Department and the Oxnard Police Department, Finkbine's boat was found in the Ventura Harbor. Investigators found that a couple had sold the boat to a Los Angeles lawyer for $47,000, well below its value of $60,000. The couple, Russel Weisse, 28, and his wife, Sally Ann, were found in Ventura County, arrested and taken to Los Angeles County to stand trial for murder. Sally Ann, 20, stood only 4 feet 4 inches high and weighed 66 pounds.

In the trial, the testimony of an accomplice, Gary Duncan, who turned state's evidence, revealed that Russel Weisse and Duncan used phoney inspector badges to board Finkbine's boat. After getting aboard, the trio pulled a gun on Finkbine and forced him to sail out of Marina del Ray to the Santa Barbara Channel. Once in the Channel, Finkbine was forced to sign transfer papers giving the Weisse's ownership of the boat.

After getting the signed papers, the trio forced Finkbine to stand on the stern of the boat. Russel Weisse then shot Finkbine with a shotgun. The blast blew him off the boat and into the ocean. Not wanting any evidence of the murder to be found, the trio retrieved Finkbine's battered body, tied weights around it and threw him back into the Channel off Ventura Harbor. The murderers did an efficient job. Finkbine's body was never found. With the possession of the ownership papers, the couple put the boat up for sale at an undervalued price in Ventura County.

After only three hours of deliberation, on October 3, 1974, the jury found Russel W. Weisse guilty of first degree murder almost a year after the tragedy. The Santa Monica Superior Court Judge sentenced Weisse to life in prison without possibility of a parole for kidnapping, armed robbery, and murder. A few weeks later in Ventura County Court, Sally Ann Weisse was found guilty of marijuana possession.

Piracy and Murder of Nicholas Church

On May 15, 1974, Nicholas A. Church left the Santa Barbara Harbor in his sailboat. On the same day Randal Wayne Dirato, 29, left the Santa Barbara Harbor in his boat. A few days later only Dirato returned, not to Santa Barbara, but to Ventura Harbor--in Church's boat. When Church did not return to Santa Barbara, he was reported missing and a search was begun. Dirato was found living aboard Church's boat in the Ventura Harbor. Dirato had sold his boat.

Dirato was arrested for piracy and murder on October 16, 1974. Authorities claimed that Dirato boarded Church's boat in the Channel, killed and disposed of him at sea and took his boat. Church was never found, dead or alive.

Piracy and Murder on the *Chronic Bitcher*

On Tuesday night, August 21, 1979, the Coast Guard received a frantic distress call from the *Chronic Bitcher* in the Channel. Santa Barbara attorney, James J. Oppen, 58, the owner, said that three heavily armed men in a 20-foot fishing boat had boarded his boat and kidnapped him. While telling that he was being tortured, the sound of gunfire was heard and Oppen's voice said, "I've been shot." The transmission ended suddenly. The Coast Guard ordered a search started immediately.

Two Coast Guard cutters, two utility boats, and a helicopter searched during the night but could not locate the boat. The next morning, the 41-foot cabin cruiser was found in Scorpion Cove at Santa Cruz Island. The *Chronic Bitcher* was adrift with its engine idling.

Oppen was found on board alone, dead of a gunshot wound to his head. The Coast Guard towed the boat to Santa Barbara Harbor where it was examined by the Sheriff's Office. Several bullet holes were found, apparently fired from inside the boat. It looked like homicide.

As a lawyer, Oppen had been heavily involved in the 1969 Union Oil Company oil spill in the Channel and had made some enemies. He had run for judge in 1976, but was not elected. His wife, Marilyn, reported that he had received several threatening telephone calls before his murder. Oppen was not in good health due to an impaired leg.

The strange distress call caused some people to wonder what really happened on board the *Chronic Bitcher*. Was it a suicide? Or was it a murder staged to confuse authorities and give the impression of a possible suicide?

Murder For Insurance

The headlines were bold, "Mother, Son Die - Effort to Save Dog Ends in Sea Tragedy." The pictures of Fred Roehler, Jr., 38, of Malibu being taken from a Coast Guard helicopter to an ambulance were dramatic and empathy provoking. But some experienced sailors became suspicious of the marine consultant's story as it unfolded in the newspapers. Except for an anonymous telephone call, Fred Roehler would have collected $820,000 in insurance money for the "accidental death" of his wife and step-son.

The tragedy began on the second day of the New Year, 1981. Fred Roehler anchored his 40 ft. yacht, *Perseverance*, at Little Scorpion Cove on the east end of Santa Cruz Island, on that fateful morning. On board was Fred Roehler, his wife Verna Jo, his stepson Douglas, Verna Jo's daughter from a previous marriage, his mother and father, two children from Roehler's previous marriage and his brother and his wife.

After lunch, Roehler, with Verna Jo, Douglas, 9, and their beagle puppy, Lady, aboard, rowed a 16 ft. dory around nearby Bird Rock to take some pictures of Douglas and the beagle with the *Perseverance* in the background. Douglas was wearing a life jacket and Roehler a "float coat." Roehler was an expert diver and a former Navy frogman. Roehler rowed the dory to the windward side of Bird Rock and while maneuvering into position to take a picture, claimed that Lady sprang at one of the sea gulls swooping around them and fell into the water. He said Douglas lunged to reach the dog, he reached over the side to get Douglas, Verna Jo shifted her position and the dory flipped over spilling all of them in the water.

Roehler said he was unable to get out from under the dory for 30 seconds to a minute because his camera strap was caught on something. When he got to the surface he said Verna Jo and

Douglas were not breathing. While treading water, he said he kept them afloat and gave them mouth to mouth resuscitation alternately, but it was difficult because the dog kept trying to climb onto his head and shoulders. Rather than put the two on top of the floating dory, he said he took them about 100 to 150 ft. upwind to Bird Rock where he put the dog ashore. He claimed he was unable to put his wife or Douglas ashore because of the rock's steepness. He continued dog paddling until a power boat, the *Sound of Music*, came by, heard him calling, and lifted them out of the water. Attempts to revive Verna Jo and Douglas were fruitless. Roehler was cold but conscious, alert and had no injuries. He was brought to the Saint Johns Hospital in Oxnard, examined and released later.

A routine autopsy was made of Verna Jo and Douglas by Dr. Craig Duncan of the Ventura County Medical Examiner-Coroner's Office and reported that they had died by accidental drowning. The case was about to be closed. Strangely, the Santa Barbara Sheriff's Office received some anonymous phone calls asking them if they knew about the unusual death of Roehler's first wife, Jean, and the large amount of insurance carried on Verna Jo and Douglas. Investigators found that Roehler's first wife had been found unconscious and face down in their swimming pool. She died a week later--never regaining consciousness. Roehler carried an accidental death insurance policy on her.

Suspicions aroused, Santa Barbara County had a second autopsy made of the two bodies by Dr. DeWitt T. Hunter, Jr. Dr. Hunter found that each had been hit in the back of their head by blows. The tragedy was no longer just another unfortunate drowning in the Channel. It looked like murder.

Fred Roehler, Jr. was arrested April 3, 1981, and charged with the murder of his wife and stepson. The trial was held in Santa Barbara County as Santa Cruz Island was in its jurisdiction.

The Santa Barbara County Prosecutor, Stanley Roden, built a strong circumstantial case around the fact that Roehler took out an accidental death portion of the insurance policy he carried on his wife only three days before she was drowned. He had taken the original insurance policy out shortly after they had married. Roehler also carried a $120,000 policy on his nine-year-old stepson. One insurance man testified that he had never heard of such a high amount being carried on a child who has no earning power to protect. Roehler was the beneficiary of $820,000, tax free, on the accidental death of his wife and stepson. Roden claimed that Roehler positioned the dory behind Bird Rock where they were out of sight of the boats anchored in Little Scorpion cove. He then hit both of them with an oar knocking them out, enabling him to drown them, and making it look like an accident. Instead of holding on to the dory to help save them, he swam 150 feet to a place on Bird Rock out of sight. The dory oars were never found.

The defense lawyers countered the Prosecution's case with a group of pathologists who claimed that the blows to the heads of the victims occurred after death and that their deaths were accidental.

On May 7, 1982, a packed courtroom waited tensely for the court clerk to read the jury's verdict. Roehler's supporters gasped and groaned when the guilty finding was read. Roehler was sentenced to prison for life.

How many more times will people use the Channel as a scene for murder or piracy? How many "accidents" have really been disguised murders?

Rapist and Mass Murderer Captured at Pelican Bay

In June of 1983, while their 32 ft. wooden sailboat *Illa Tika* was in drydock in Ensenada, Mexico, Owen and Angelica Handy met a man who called himself Angel Jackson. The Handys, enroute to San Francisco, took Jackson on as a non-paid deck hand. In July, on their way north, they stopped off at Santa Barbara to pick up drinking water. Jackson rowed a dinghy ashore and went swimming by himself at a nearby nude beach. By this time, the Handys were feeling uncomfortable with their black sailor. He was not much of a sailor and was seasick for most of the voyage from Mexico. He told them that he was an artist from Philadelphia looking for work.

The Handys then sailed their shabby boat to Pelican Bay on the north side of Santa Cruz Island. They spent several weeks anchored in the bay, lolling in the sun and reportedly bumming liquor from other boaters.

On July 30, 1983, a couple who owned the *Yankee Rebel II*, a nearby boat, invited Jackson aboard for dinner. At about 11 p.m., after the husband had gone to bed, Jackson pulled a knife on the woman and raped her in the boat's salon.

Just before dawn the next day, after Jackson had gone, the woman told her husband what had happened. He radioed the Coast Guard and reported his wife's rape. The Santa Barbara County Sheriff's Special Enforcement Team embarked on the Coast Guard cutter *Point Judith* as the man reported that guns were on board the boat where the assailant was staying.

The cutter dropped off an inflatable boat with three deputies and a Coast Guard crew member before entering Pelican Bay. When Jackson saw the two vessels approaching the *Illa Tika*, he jumped into the water and swam to a dinghy tied to another yacht in the bay. He started paddling for shore. As the deputies changed course to intercept Jackson, the rape victim warned them that he had a knife around his neck.

After Jackson's dinghy caught in the kelp, he threw his knife overboard before being captured. A member of the Sheriff's dive team recovered his rusty wooden-handled pocket knife from the bottom of the bay for evidence.

The rapist was taken back to Santa Barbara aboard the *Point Judith* and the rape victim was helicoptered to the Goleta Valley Community Hospital for treatment. While being interviewed at the sheriff's office, she saw a wanted poster on the wall and cried out, "Oh my God, that's the guy who raped me."

It was Kevin Cooper, wanted in San Bernardino county for the murder of Chino Hills residents F. Douglas and Peg Ryan, their daughter, Jessica, and a young guest, Christopher Hughes. He was also wanted for the attempted murder of the Ryan's eight-year-old son, Joshua, who survived having his throat slit.

Cooper had escaped from Chino State Prison just days before murdering the Ryan family. He had not been seen by authorities since.

Boaters interviewed at Pelican Bay said that the yachting world is informal and it is not unusual to pick up strangers as deck hands. The Handys had heard of the Chino massacre on their radio, but had not associated Angel Jackson with Kevin Cooper. Later the couple said that they were grateful to be alive and thankful Cooper hadn't harmed them. They were very lucky.

Cooper was subsequently tried and found guilty of murder in 1985. He was sentenced to life in prison without parole.

Channel Boat Thieves

Channel thieves will steal small and large boats-even from authorities. In April of 1983, Ljudevit Blazevic, returned from a trip to find his new Formosa 46 ft. sailboat had been stolen. The owner had planned to live on board the boat valued at $120,000. The boat was so new that Blazevic hadn't had time to paint a name on it.

During the evening of August 27, 1985, the wife of a Ventura Harbor patrolman, picking up her husband, discovered the 24 ft. rescue boat was missing. In the search for the boat the patrolemen grabbed a 21-year-old scrambling off the boat which was found about a 100 yards away. The man was arrested for allegedly stealing the Harbor Patrol rescue boat.

Pot Boat Stolen From U. S. Customs

Their suspicions aroused, the U. S. Coast Guard arrested three men and one woman aboard the 60 ft. sloop *Mir* off San Miguel Island on November 22, 1984. The crew found eight tons of marijuana on board valued at $6.7 million. A radio check made after boarding the vessel revealed that the *Mir* had been stolen from a U. S. Customs warehouse a year earlier.

In March of 1985, the skipper of the *Mir* and apparent leader of the group, Richard Dobson of Texas, was sentenced to seven years in prison. He had served time before for smuggling. The others received lesser sentences.

Aerial view of Ventura Harbor

Aerial view of Ventura Harbor

ELEVEN

BOATING AND DIVING ACCIDENTS
1970 To 1980

$\mathbf{S}$erious boating accidents reported in the 1970s jumped to 163, an 80% rise over the 90 accidents reported for the previous decade. Sixty-six deaths resulted from the boating accidents and more than 424 people were rescued. Of the 163 boats involved in serious accidents: 43 sank; 83 ran aground, capsized or caught fire; and seven collided with other vessels or an object in the Channel. An estimated 133 boats were destroyed.

In the 1970s, deaths from diving (26) and swimming (50) totaled 76, a great increase over the 22 for the previous decade. With the deaths of 13 people from aircraft and helicopters accidents in the Channel, a reported total of 155 people perished in the Channel, almost double the 60s figure of 81.

Power and Sailboat Accidents

Of the 163 vessels having serious accidents during the 1970s, 109 were identified as power boats and 35 as sailboats. Fifty-two or 32% of the vessels were small boats (23 ft. or smaller). Seventeen of the 35 sailboats and 29 of the 109 power boats were small boats. From 1970 thru 1981, a total of 205 boats were involved in serious accidents in which 137 were identified as power boats and 49 as sailboats.

117

Loss of *Rosamond*

One of the first major tragedies of the 1970s occurred on a small sailboat. Superior Court Judge West paid with his life for being in the Channel in rough weather with too small a boat. A lawyer friend, Hugh Gallagher, also lost his life in the capsizing of West's 21 ft. sloop *Rosamond* at Frenchy's Cove on Anacapa Island. A third man on board, Douglas Deihl, a county marshal, narrowly escaped with his life.

The three men left Channel Islands Harbor on a Saturday morning in April 1970 for Anacapa. About three quarters of the way to Anacapa, the winds increased in velocity and the seas tossed the small boat about roughly dismasting it. The small sloop was not designed for the Channels high winds and choppy seas. Using the small outboard engine, West got the sloop to Frenchy's Cove and threw over the anchor. By this time the winds were over thirty knots and the surf was smashing loudly against the nearby rocky cliffs. The small anchor would not hold in the winds and tugging seas. This time the small outboard engine would not start. It was now about 3:30 p.m.

As the men frantically tried to start the engine, the waves carried them close to the cliffs. A huge wave "sloshing white water 20 to 25 feet high, picked the boat up and turned it upside down." The men in the surging water scrambled to save their lives. All wore life jackets.

Douglas Deihl made it to the rocky shore where he reached out to grab the other two men drifting by him. He could not quite reach their extended arms. West and Gallagher continued down wind out of sight.

Deihl, tired and depressed, sought what little shelter there was in the tiny, rocky cove. It was a lonely and cold night. The next morning around eight o'clock some fisherman came by and rescued him. The Coast Guard initiated an extensive search, but never found West's body. Several weeks later Gallagher's body was found miles out to sea from Anacapa Island. The Coast Guard terminated the search for West on April 15, 1970.

Proud *La Jenelle* Meets Her Fate

The most spectacular tragedy of the 1970s was the beaching of *La Jenelle* in a savage Channel storm. The proud passenger liner, *La Jenelle*, built in 1929, was showing her age, but still had trim lines when she met an ignominious death in the Channel. The handsome, but rusting 12,500 ton, 465 ft. long ship, had a rich history of carrying passengers between Miami and the Bahamas before World War II. Known as the *Bahama Star* in the Caribbean, she was a popular and glamorous ship.

With the entry of the United States into the War, *La Jenelle*, like many other passenger liners, was drafted into service. She carried troops in the Mediterranean Sea, the Pacific, and made voyages to the Baltic countries. Many attempts were made on her life, but she escaped torpedos and bombings and was nicknamed the *Lucky Star*.

After the War, she was converted back to civilian status and continued the Bahama cruises until the 1960s. In 1959, a disastrous fire on another cruise ship, the *Yarmouth Castle,* unfortunately, changed her pleasant life style. The *Castle's* fire killed 165 people and injured many more. In the following investigations, maritime regulations were changed requiring extensive alterations on cruise ships like the *Bahama Star*. The *Star* owners looked at the cost of the alterations and decided it was not economically feasible. The *Star* was pulled out of service when deadlines for required improvements were reached in December of 1968.

The *Star* was put up for sale and sold to the Western Steamship Co. She was renamed the *La Jenelle* and sailed through the Panama Canal to the Pacific where she was to be sold again. The *La Jenelle* was anchored about one and three quarter miles off Port Hueneme on August 12, 1968, to await her next adventure. The sea served as a used boat lot for her.

Neglected, the *Jenelle* forlornly faced the Channel's fierce winds and waves, swinging on her anchor to each change of direction. She was not a graceful sight tethered to a solidary chain, going nowhere and serving an unfamiliar useless role.

Forewarnings of tragedy appeared in November of 1969. While prospective buyers were examining her, their shore boat broke its line and drifted toward shore. Crewmen launched one of the *La Jenelle's* 20 ft. life boats to save the drifting boat. Both boats were lost.

A month later on December 18, 1969, two of the crew members on board the *La Jenelle* were drowned when their 18 ft. shore boat capsized tossing them into the rough surf. A short time later another small boat tied to the *Jenelle* broke lose and drifted out to sea toward Anacapa Island. The Coast Guard, this time, successfully caught and towed the boat to safety.

The *Jenelle* finally fell victim to one of the Channel's fierce storms on April 13, 1970. Winds were raging up to 65 miles per hour and waves were running 10 ft. high and more. The high winds and pounding waves forced the helpless ship slowly toward shore and her death. The crew onboard had little warning of the coming catastrophe. Within 23 minutes, due to the anchor dragging or

Navy helicopter rescues two men from *La Jenelle* in 1969.

the line breaking, the now unlucky *Jenelle* slammed intoSilver Strand Beach, just west of the entrance to Port Hueneme Harbor. Two crew members were still onboard and in danger of losing their lives. The two men attempted to save the ship by pumping out the bilges. After working for about four hours, and with the ship listing badly to port, they realized it was hopeless and decided to abandon ship. One of the crewmen, Lester Ellis, suffered from exposure and was unable to get into the open enabling a helicopter pilot to lift him off the ship. Only after great skill by Navy helicopter pilot, LCDR Dick Shand from Point Mugu, were the two men safely lifted off in the gusting, dangerous winds.

Later, at the dispensary at Port Hueneme Navy Base, Ellis explained why he hadn't left earlier when offered help: "I loved that ship and I did not want to let her go until I had to. All I was thinking about was staying with the ship."

Shipwrecks

The *La Jenelle* lay sadly on her side shuddering as each pounding wave hit her. It was not a pleasant sight. Feelings ran high to "save her." She continued to deteriorate in the surf, however, as the owners could not decide what course to take. Numerous proposals were considered, including salvaging and making a fishing pier out of her. Inaction by the owners and authorities prevented any practical solution from evolving. The Channel's winds and seas resolved the issue. Her hull became so damaged by waves and so full of sand that it became economically impossible to save her.

The *La Jenelle* now lies in her grave next to the entrance to Port Hueneme and at the east end of Silver Strand Beach. Visitors walk on top of her without knowing the proud ship is under their feet. She now serves ignominiously as part of the harbor breakwater. No monument marks her grave or her civilian and war time

La Jenelle lies on her side next to the Port Hueneme jetty, 1970.
(Star-Free Press photo)

feats. A sad ending for the once sleek 465 ft. ship that served her country and many happy vacationers so well.

Power Yacht Accidents

During a stormy day on November 16, 1970, the 27 ft. cabin cruiser, *Therapy*, with five passengers aboard, became engulfed in an angry channel surf at the entrance to the Ventura Harbor. One wave flipped the *Therapy* upside down. A second wave flipped the boat right side up, but unfortunately the passengers could not hold on and were dumped into the raging surf. One passenger was drowned, but four were rescued. The body of the dead person was not recovered until the next day.

Patrol Boat Sinks

On November 28th, 1970, attempting to rescue three people on a sailboat that had run aground at the Ventura Harbor entrance, the patrol boat was smashed against the breakwater

Shipwrecks

La Jenelle at Port Hueneme May 1970. (U.S. Navy photo)

Present day remains of *La Jenelle*. (Star-Free Press)

rocks and demolished. The crew of the sailboat and the patrol boat were both rescued.

Four days before Christmas in 1973, another 23 ft. Ventura Harbor patrol boat capsized and sank at the entrance while trying to reach a 42 ft. ketch that had run aground on the beach. Three men were rescued from the patrol boat and the ketch. The accident was blamed on some large freak waves.

Rescue Off Point Conception

After hitting something in the water while motoring off Point Conception the night of July 14, 1975, two men and a woman were forced to abandon their sinking 42 ft. cabin cruiser. After the collision water started flowing into the boat and the three people started bailing for their life. Robert Peterson reported later, "We had two bilge pumps going full blast, but both burned out...I was trying to steer and radio at the same time and he was bailing."

A large ship came within 60 yards of their boat at about 2:30 a.m. and shined a light on them. The cabin cruiser flashed several desperate SOS signals to the ship. After receiving some recognition signals back, Peterson said, "They flashed us a message of some kind with their lights and then just split. . . .It was incredible, a heartbreak."

Between five and 5:30 p.m., with the wind blowing about 30 knots, the three frightened people climbed into the pitching life raft and cast off just in time. The boat sank immediately leaving them very much alone in the rough seas.

As they bobbed about like a cork drifting aimlessly, planes passed over them six times but did not see them. After drifting toward Santa Cruz Island for hours, an abalone boat, the *Blue Angel,* saw their waving and rescued them. The *Blue Angel* was a real angel in disguise to them.

Coast Guard Cutter Damaged

On March 26, 1975, when Joseph Cardoza's 22 ft. sailboat was sighted floundering and in danger of sinking in the Channel, the *China Clipper*, a fishing boat, came alongside Cardoza's boat to assist him. In the process of transferring the family to the *Clipper* in fifty knots winds and frightning waves, Cardoza's foot was crushed between the two boats. The *Clipper* radioed the Coast Guard to pick up Cardoza.

On the return to port after picking up Cardoza, the 41 ft. cutter was hit by such powerful waves that its "storm proof" cabin windows were smashed. The cutter was so badly damaged that it was nearly sunk by incoming waves. The cutter put in to Oxnard later for repair work.

Fishing Boat Tragedies

More than 30 fishing boats were sunk or involved in serious accidents from 1970 thru 1981 in the Channel. At least seven fishermen died in the accidents and over 132 were rescued from sinking or capsized fishing boats. In the same storm that claimed the *La Jenelle,* a 36 ft. abalone boat and the 40 ft. fishing boat, *Sea Devil*, collided with each other off Santa Barbara. A Coast Guard helicopter was called in and rescued five from the damaged boats. Another large fishing boat was the victim of a hit and run by an ocean going vessel in the Channel on midnight of Feb. 27, 1974. Luckily, the boat survived.

Chelan and *Sansiena II* Collision

The 58 ft. trawler, *Chelan,* was not so lucky on the night of Feb. 26, 1978. In clear weather and calm seas, about two miles off Santa Cruz Island, the *Chelan* got in the path of the 810 ft. long tanker *Sansiena II*. In the following collision, the *Chelan* went down, but the tanker crew stopped the huge ship and rescued the seven crewmen.

After an investigation of the accident by the Coast Guard, it was ruled that the *Chelan* was at fault. The fishing boat had: 1. Failed to keep clear of the tanker, which had the right of way; 2. Failed to carry a proper masthead light; 3. Not properly shielded its stern light; 4. Not crossed the shipping lane at right angles; 5. Not kept a proper look out; and 6. Failed to keep running lights on or they were obscured.

Pioneer and *Sansiena II* Collision

For some unknown reason the crew of the 42 ft. sport fishing boat, *Pioneer*, did not see the enormous hull of the tanker *Sansiena II* and rammed its bow into it. The collision occurred at about 5:50 a.m. on Sept. 19, 1973, near Anacapa Island. The bow of the *Pioneer* was badly damaged, but the boat managed to return safely to port with its ten passengers and crew.

Sunset Loses Its Fish

A few nights later, on Sept. 22, 1973, the 85 ft. commercial fishing boat *Sunset*, while returning to port with a full load of fish, ran aground on the beach off McGrath State Park. The helicopter called was able to lift the crew of seven sucessfully off the stricken vessel.

The boat's captain, Milton Wolf, said later, "I don't know whether the man at the wheel fell asleep or not, but he should have seen the beach."

Once the boat was disabled in the surf, the boat filled with water and the fish flowed out into the ocean. News of the free

Sunset aground September 1973.(Star-Free Press)

lunch spread rapidly to the bird community. Seagulls and other species hovered about the wreck for days freeloading on the fish.

Another 45 ft. commercial fishing boat ran aground at Pierpont Beach at 10:30 PM on August 10, 1974. This time the engines failed and caused the accident. No one was hurt.

Fishing boats sank in a variety of places under different conditions. A 20 ft. abalone boat burned and sank off Coal Oil Pt. on June 10, 1971. Another sank off San Miguel Island in which one died and two were rescued. In May of 1975 the *Ann* caught fire and broke up at night in the Channel. Somehow the hull remained afloat, a danger to other vessels in the Channel. Two men were rescued. A 30 ton fishing boat selected a convenient location for its crewmen to sink, in the Santa Barbara harbor.

The *Monte Carlo*, a sport fishing boat, came close to becoming a sinking victim of the Channel. Between Santa Cruz Island and Santa Barbara, the *Monte Carlo* sprang a leak and was taking on water fast. The crew transferred the 26 passengers to another boat and returned to port to repair the damage.

In 1976, the 80 ft. *Lucy Ann* sank in 130 ft. of water near oil platform Heidi because of too much success. The vessel, estimated to be worth over $200,000, became overloaded from a huge catch of bonita and floundered. The crew of twelve men were spotted soon after and rescued. In May of 1978, a 40 ft. commercial fishing boat burned and sank off Goleta. The crew also were successfully rescued.

The *Three Sisters*

The four man crew of the commercial fishing boat *Three Sisters* were not so lucky. The 36 ft. boat left Channel Islands Harbor on Tuesday, January 5, 1982, for San Miguel Island to catch rock cod. Nothing was ever heard of the *Three Sisters* again except for a mysterious radio message to the Coast Guard on Saturday from a "Land-based radio operator" who said the *Three Sisters* was anchored and safe at Santa Rosa Island. It wasn't.

When the ship was reported overdue, the Coast Guard started an extensive search covering over 4,000 square miles between San Miguel Island and Point Conception. On Sunday, January 9th, the body of one of the crew, Isidro Ramirez, was found floating in his life jacket near some debris about three miles from San Miguel Island. Another fishing boat, the *Pacific Sun,* found the body. No signs of the *Three Sisters* or the other three crewmen were found.

Months later on April Fool,s Day, 1982, a skeleton was found near Simonton Cove on San Miguel Island by Chief Ranger Robert Arnberger, of the Channel Islands National Park staff. The body was later identified as one of the crew members. The bodies of the other missing fishermen have never been found. The cause of the *Three Sister's* sinking still remains a mystery.

El Capitan's Collision

The 50 ft. trawler *El Capitan* was about six miles offshore from Ventura on December 23, 1981, when it encountered a big freighter in the Channel around 2:20 in the morning. The fishing boat had been to Anacapa and was returning to port with 500 lbs. of shrimp on board. The *El Capitan* was nearly out of the north bound shipping lane when disaster hit. The Captain, Dana Enlow, said, "I thought we were safe. The ship was behind us off to the portside." Enlow learned that the speed of big ocean going ships can be deceiving.

About fifteen minutes went by when, "We heard a tremendous crash off the starboard bow. Then we got sucked against the ship and it scraped us the whole way until it went by. I didn't know if we were going to be sucked into the propellers or not."

Enlow tried to contact the freighter by radio, but to no avail. He could get no response on two frequencies. The freighter kept going as if nothing had happened. As the *El Capitan* was badly damaged and starting to sink, Enlow called the Coast Guard and gave their position. Enlow said, "We knew it was just a matter of minutes before it would sink. We put on life preservers and got out the life raft and threw some empty boxes over. Then we jumped in and swam away from the boat."

The crew of three paused about 20 yards away from the boat and watched it sink. It was only ten minutes after the freighter had rammed them. The men said it was eerie watching the *El Capitain* go down with the engine room lights shinning underwater as the boat disappeared.

Thinking they were safe until picked up, the men got another shock. The wind had blown them back into the shipping lane. The crew set off flares to warn ships of their presence. They could see a big tanker bearing down on them in the dark. Realizing the danger, the Coast Guard radioed the tanker and had it slow down. The three men were rescued about an hour after their boat sank. Unfortunately, the commercial fishing boat was not insured for its replacement value of $206,000—not much of a Christmas gift for the owner. Fortunately, the crew had been saved. It is not always so. A Coast Guard spokesman said that it was "not uncommon" for ocean going freighters and tankers to hit a small boat and not realize it. Boater beware.

Diving Boat and Diver Accidents

Four urchin divers in their 25 ft. boat came close to becoming Channel victims in September of 1976. Their boat flipped over in rough seas tossing the men in the cold water. During their thirteen hours in the water waiting to be rescued, they had some strange encounters with the Channel's inhabitants. One of the divers said, "two whales came close to us, but just looked around and left." A few sharks also inspected the men, but did not attack.

The *Intruder's* Ordeal

The three man crew on the 43 ft. urchin diving boat, *Intruder,* had been working together for over five years. When the boat left Channel Islands Harbor for San Nicolas Island on January 6, 1982, the men had no knowledge that the feared east winds were going to strike the Channel. The divers harvested more than 7,500 pounds of sea urchins, a good haul, for sale to a Ventura firm, who packs and ships them to Japan.

About 4:00 p.m. on Thursday, January 7th, the divers started back on what is normally an eight hour trip. Luboff, the owner, said they realized it would be a longer and rougher trip back because of the high northeast winds that had come up. Luboff said, "We hadn't expected this easterly condition to be so strong."

About midnight crewman, Mendenhall, went below and found water coming into the forward section. Attempts to stop the leak were not working so Luboff radioed the Coast Guard for help. Within twenty minutes a helicopter found them, 25 miles north of San Nicolas Island, and lowered a bilge pump. It was not sufficient to stem the flow.

The *Canberra*, an Australian destroyer, hearing the call for help came alongside in case the crew wanted assistance. The seas were so high the *Canberra* did not dare come too close for fear of smashing the smaller boat. As the divers worked to save the *Intruder,* two more Coast Guard vessels arrived on the scene at around 2:00 a.m.: the 41 ft. cutter from Channel Islands Harbor and the 82 ft. cutter *Point Carrew* from Santa Barbara. By about 4:00 a.m. it became clear that the *Intruder* was not going to be saved. The waves and winds of the Channel were too much to combat. One by one, the three divers jumped off the floundering boat and swam for the nearby cutter. Tired, but happy to be alive, the three were returned to Channel Islands Harbor. Jeff Luboff said, "We kidded each other a little about things that happened, ...But no one was making jokes last night at all. We could joke this morning, but not last night."

Towing Tragedy

While at least 32 divers died in underwater accidents from 1970 thru 1981, perhaps the most tragic occurred to two young divers as their 17 ft. Boston Whaler was being towed to safety by the Coast Guard. Stephen White, 23, from Port Hueneme and Charles Lang, 20, from Ventura had been scuba diving in Smugglers Cove at Santa Cruz Island on December 15, 1977. Around 5:00 p.m., not being able to start their engine, the two men called the Coast Guard for a tow back to Channel Islands Harbor. A 41 ft. Coast Guard vessel responded to the call and commenced to tow them.

The two divers put on their wet suits and life preservers and remained in the Boston Whaler for the trip to port. The Whaler was towed about 100 ft. behind the Coast Guard cutter. The tow seemed to proceed uneventfully for the three hour trip--until the cutter made a sweeping turn to enter the Channel Islands Harbor. At that point, the cutter's crew saw that the Whaler had overturned and the two men were not visible.

The Coast Guard initiated a search in the night but could not find the two men. At first the cutter's crew said they checked the condition of the two men every ten minutes by flashlight and that the divers must be near the harbor entrance. A 225 mile search pattern was made by helicopter and boats for the missing men.

With the water temperature at 61 degrees and rough seas, little hope was given for finding the men alive.

The following day about 11:00 a.m., the search helicopter found one body about seven miles southwest of Channel Islands Harbor. The cutter, *Point Evans,* found the second body an hour later. The men no longer had on their life preservers or the top of their wet suits. Speculation ran high as to what had happened. The Coast Guard cutter crew were thought to have been negligent. If the towing crew had checked every ten minutes why were the diver's bodies seven miles away from the entrance?

Many surmised that the cutter had towed the Whaler too fast and had caused it to flip over in the rough seas. The error was compounded by the crew not keeping a constant check on the small boat. The men probably held on to the Whaler hoping the crew would notice their plight. The force of waves must have torn off their life preservers and the top of their wet suits. Chilled from the cold and fatigued from the pounding of the waves, the two young men were forced to let go and to die of exposure and drowning.

Havoc From The Winds of 1976

Fierce winds hit the Channel basin during 1976. The first major blow occurred April 19-20, when winds reached hurricane velocity. The winds blew a steady 55 to 60 knots in the Channel Islands Harbor, with spurts in the county of 90 mph. Bob Besett of the National Park Service reported that winds exceeded 100 mph on Santa Barbara Island. Besett said, "The gauges went plumb off the chart." One wind indicator actually tore itself apart when the winds exceeded 100 mph.

The small boats that were caught in the high winds suffered the most. The *Sure Bet,* a 22 ft. open motor boat, was lost off Anacapa Island. It was found later, bottom up, off Palos Verdes Peninsula, miles away. Six people were missing and presumed dead.

Fierce Winds of November 1976

During the weekend of November 28, 1976, winds swept across the Channel shortly after midnight on Saturday night of the 28th causing misery to boaters. A Channel Islands Harbor spokesman said the winds were blowing at a steady 70 mph with gusts to 90 mph.

The Coast Guard reported that around 40 boats called for assistance and that an estimated 100 persons were rescued by Coast Guard and U.S. Navy helicopters near Santa Cruz and Anacapa Islands. On the first day of the 'Santana' wind, two boats were known to have sunk and six more were missing and presumed sunk. Another 10 boats were leaking badly and in danger of sinking. Over 40 people received hospital treatment for injuries.

After the winds hit, the Ken family, aboard their 62 ft. sailboat at Santa Cruz Island, put out a total of four anchors. The winds snapped all four lines and blew the helpless boat ashore. Ken reported that four other boats in their anchorage were smashed against the rocks and destroyed. The Ken boat was valued at $200,000.

A Coronado 25 sailboat was picked up by one wave in Pelican Bay at Santa Cruz Island, and was tossed fiercely against the rocks. Witnesses said the boat hit the rocks with such a strong force that it was demolished with one blow.

At least 45 victims were flown to the mainland from the islands by helicopter. One victim, forced to abandon his craft, floated in the cold ocean all night until picked up by the Coast Guard. The man was still conscious, but in poor condition. Another sailboat was found sailing efficiently in rough seas 60 miles west of Santa Cruz Island, without a crew. The crew had been swept overboard by the strong wind and seas.

In describing the force of the winds, a rescue helicopter pilot said that it took him only seven minutes to get to Santa Cruz Island from the mainland, but it took 45 minutes to return.

During the second day of the 'Santana,' eight boaters were rescued off Anacapa, 15 more distress calls were received, two boats capsized, two boats ran into a harbor jetty and another cabin cruiser sank in its slip without attempting to face the ocean waves. At Little Scorpion Cove on Santa Cruz Island it was so rough that a 30 ft. sailboat was flipped end over end until it crashed against the shore rocks.

Storm wave breaking over Ventura Harbor entrance jetty.

The *Skippy*'s Brief But Deadly Encounter

The 40 ft. cabin cruiser, *Skippy*, became a victim of the Channel's fierce northeast winds and an overly friendly sailboat. It was calm and peaceful near Prisoner's Cove at Santa Cruz Island where the *Skippy* was anchored Saturday, November, 28, 1976. The four people on board the *Skippy* had a lesurely barbeque and turned in early Saturday evening. Around midnight a feared 'Santana' wind swept across the Channel from the northeast. Like hundreds of other boats at the Islands for the weekend, the *Skippy* was caught unprepared by the sudden 50 knot winds.

Richard Box, on board the *Skippy*, said, "The wind was incredible. Waves were throwing us in all directions. Even then several boats were on the rocks."

A nearby sailboat, with two couples and a dog on board, lost its anchor in the blow and swung about into the *Skippy*. To save themselves, the frightened sailboat crew clung to the *Skippy* for protection. Box upset with the situation said, "They were grinding us to pieces. I yelled at their skipper to pull off our bow, but he refused. He was using us for an anchor."

Fearing for the safety of his own crew and boat, Box tore off the boats heavy VHF antenae, and with a few select maritime oaths, started hitting the sailboat's skipper over the head with it when the sailboat veered near him. Unfortunately, the *Skippy* had been damaged badly by the hammering of the sailboat and was taking in water. Box called the Coast Guard for assistance when he realized the extent of the damage. Finally, the sailboat crew pulled away from the *Skippy*. No sooner had the Coast Guard arrived and had taken the four aboard the cutter, the boat started sinking and was abandoned. The Coast Guard commander refused to tow the boat.

After the storm, Box returned to Prisoners looking to salvage the *Skippy,* if possible. But the boat was not where it had been abandoned. Although badly damaged, the boat seemed to have a will of her own. The *Skippy* apparently decided to explore the Channel underworld. The boat continued moving with the currents, bouncing off the bottom as she drifted along Santa Cruz under water. Eventually, a passing diving boat, the *Coral Sea,* saw the *Skippy's* cabin top near the surface and towed the boat to shore. Box and his friends later salvaged most of their possessions off the vessel. Box was last seen searching the coast for a blue hulled fiberglass sailboat with two couples and a Weimaraner dog on board--the villains who caused his boat to sink.

The persistent Box found the sailboat owner and sued him for damages and the loss of his boat. He was almost sorry because the expensive lawsuit took seven years to settle.

Fog

Not as noisy as Basin winds, but just as awesome are Channel fogs. Fog forms in the Channel with a frightening suddenness that disturbs the most seasoned sailor. It is especially eerie to be crossing the shipping lanes, hear fog horns and wonder how close the unseen vessel is to you. In an unexpected fog of August 24, 1975, an estimated 40 boats were guided into the Ventura Harbor by the Coast Guard and Harbor Patrol. Two boats missed the Channel Islands Harbor entrance and ran aground. Many other sudden fogs have caused panic among boat crews close to harbor entrances.

Tragedies and Rescues at Ventura's Harbor Entrance

On November 17, 1975, a dentist was unsuccessful in getting his 33 ft. sport fishing boat through the Ventura Harbor entrance. Dr. Harry Rosenfeld, 40, with his 13-year-old son on board, broached his boat in the entrance swells. The waves swept the boat into the breakwater jetty with a tremendous wallop, but the father and son were rescued. Both were injured in the accident and hospitalized for a short time. The boat was badly damaged by the confrontation with the jetty rocks.

The doctor blamed the Port District for the accident and filed suit against the District on January 13, 1976, for over $370,000

Sailboat forced on the beach near Ventura Harbor. One of three boats wrecked in January 1977. (Star-Free Press)

for general damages and injuries suffered in the boat grounding. It took nearly six years for the case to work its way through the slow moving civil court system. Finally, in September of 1981, a Superior Court jury ruled in favor of the Ventura Port District and against the dentist. Many similar cases have been filed against the District.

Helicopter Rescue

The Ventura County Sheriff Department, Coast Guard and Navy helicopter pilots, as the harbor patrols, have consistently been available when needed and made daring and courageous rescues of boaters. Many rescues have occurred near the entrance to Ventura Harbor. One of the most spectacular took place on January 21, 1974.

Unable to maneuver in the pounding surf at the Ventura Harbor entrance, a 20 ft. sailboat had capsized spilling the crew of two into the surf. A Sheriff helicopter pilot, Collins, hovered over the victims and lowered deputy sheriff Mike Mason into the

Sheriff deputy rescuing boaters at Ventura Harbor entrance, January 1974. (Star-Free Press photo)

surf to rescue the victims. Mason managed to secure a line to the one of the crew who was seen struggling in the water. Collins lifted him out to safety. The copter crew was too late to rescue the second seaman who drowned.

Sadly, a few years later, Collins crashed and lost his life when he inadvertently hit a power cable stretched across a canyon during a fire fighting mission.

Harbor District Accidents

Harbor Master Office personnel in the two counties write up a report for each reported accident in or near the entrance of their facility. In a review of Ventura Harbor accidents from October 1977 thru 1981, the Ventura Harbor Master received 1,165 distress calls and towed 864 vessels to safety. The Harbor Patrol lost two of their own rescue boats in making rescues of other boats at the often dangerous entrance. During this four year plus period, 206 boats ran aground within or near the entrance, 68 sank, 68 capsized and 18 had collisions. A total of 60 people were injured and seven drowned.

Total Channel Shipwrecks and Accidents

During 1980 and 1981, 46 major boating accidents occurred in which seven people died, at least nine were injured, and 67 rescued. Of the 46 vessels involved, 16 sank and 24 capsized, ran aground, or burned.

An additional six divers and 15 swimmers died from drowning. Six aircraft and helicopter accidents contributed another 10 deaths to the toll for a total of 39 Channel deaths in the two year period. Nearly 100 were rescued. If boat use continues to grow and the death rate for the first two years continues to be the same for the remainder of the decade, 195 to 250 deaths will occur, hundreds more will be injured, and more than 335 to 450 people will be rescued.

Ships and Boats

The Channel has taken a heavy toll of vessels and people. From 1754 to 1982 more than 470 shipwrecks and major vessel accidents occurred in which someone was killed or several were badly injured. Over 272 people died in these accidents. The number of injured must run over a thousand, although records available do not reflect this. Of the 470 major accidents, some 428 vessels were destroyed; 226 boats sank; 155 capsized; and at least twelve large and 183 small boat collisions took place.

Diving and Swimming

A total of 124 deaths occurred from diving (37), swimming (82), and from people drowning in cars plunging into the Channel.

Aircraft

Seventeen aircraft and helicopter crashes claimed the lives of 34 people in the Channel. The bodies of many of these victims have never been found.

Total Casualties

Up to 1982, a total of 431 people were reported killed in the Channel from ships and assorted barges and vessels, diving, swimming and aircraft accidents, and murder. Luckily, thousands of people were rescued. Hundreds more have been pulled from possible disasters that were never reported.

What Can Be Done?

Knowing that perhaps another 200 to 250 boats will be destroyed in the next decade, 195 to 250 people killed, and hundreds more injured in Channel accidents, is it now time to do something? But what?

No recreational boat operator in California is required to pass a test or to have a license to operate a boat from the size of a dinghy to a huge power yacht. While a minimum age exists to operate a car, none exists to operate a recreational boat of any size. While many boat dealers are providing instruction to boat buyers, perhaps it is time to require formal testing of an operator's knowledge of sea rules and skills. It is very likely that accidents would be reduced if boat operators were required to have knowledge of the Channel's weather behavior and patterns.

Here he lies where he longed to be;
Home is the sailor, home from the sea,
And the hunter home from the hill.

Elegy on Robert Louis Stevenson's tomb in Somoa.

TWELVE

AIRCRAFT ACCIDENTS AND UNEXPLAINED HAPPENINGS - 1970s & 1980s

The Disappearing 'Blip'

The incident did occur on April Fool's Day, April 1, 1970, but the event was real. Senior Chief Petty Officer, H. W. Shigley, Commander of the Point Hueneme Coast Guard Station, received a call from the Point Mugu Naval Air Station beacon around six in the evening. Personnel at the beacon reported seeing a "distress blip" on their radar screen indicating an airplane had crashed in the Channel. Seconds after seeing the distress signal, the men operating the beacon claimed they saw a "fire flare up and a cloud of smoke" in the sea about three miles from the Ventura Harbor entrance.

Based on the report from the Naval Station, three Coast Guard cutters, two Coast Guard helicopters, and a crash boat rushed to the accident location from Pt. Mugu. The crash area was searched thoroughly for two hours but no trace of wreckage was found.

While flying its search pattern over the sea, a Coast Guard helicopter did come across a disabled boat blinking flashlights frantically at them. The copter radioed the boat's position to a searching cutter which went to their aid. Three people were on board the craft. Their engine had stopped running while the boat was in mid channel. An unexplained 'blip' saved the trio from a possible tragedy in the Channel.

What really happened to the 'blip'? The flashing lights from the disabled boat did not explain the 'sighting' on the beacon scope. The reported plane crash was never resolved by authorities. No planes were reported missing for the next few days. Could it have been smugglers not wishing to identify their activities or their missing plane?

Plunging Cessna

A similar mystery occurred ten years later except that the wreckage of the plane was found. About one o'clock in the afternoon of January 14, 1980, a Cessna 207-U was approaching the Santa Barbara Airport from the Channel in heavy rain. On board the craft was the lodge leader of 20,000 California Masons, Hermon Heffron, his wife, and four other people. One of the passengers, Don Dockendorf, was a former Santa Barbara City Councilman.

About 50 seconds after the plane had received clearance to land, and was on its landing approach, the Cessna suddenly disappeared from the radar screen, a FAA spokesman reported. A search was quickly ordered.

The first sign of the plane's wreckage was a woman's purse in the water. Debris was spread over a two mile area. The parts of two bodies were found. Sharks were also active in the area of the debris.

The Cessna had plunged into the sea about four miles off Gaviota, north of Santa Barbara. One authority said, "We don't know if they had engine trouble or whatever, but all of a sudden they dropped off the radar." Another Channel mystery that may never be solved.

Aerocommander Vanishes

On March 1, 1978, the Security Air Transport Service was flying four prisoners, including one woman and three men, from Santa Maria to Santa Barbara on a short flight. The pilot radioed the Santa Barbara Airport control tower from his twin engine Aerocommander that he was over Gaviota and preparing to land. Suddenly, as in the Cessna 207-U case, the tower lost radio contact with the plane. The Aerocommander and its seven passengers vanished. Poor weather prevented a quick search, but no wreckage was found when a search was made.

Later the wreckage of the plane was found in the mountains miles inland from the airport. No one knows what really caused the accident. Could the prisoners have attempted to overpower the guard and pilot?

Missing Body Reappears

On February 2, 1980, Jerry Lively and Raymond Bouse were flying low over the water, about 25 ft. high, along the Ventura coast in a Piper Colt. The plane appeared to lose power and then plunged nose down into the ocean 200 yards offshore between Hollywood Beach and Oxnard Shores. A witness to the crash, Mary Davis, happened to be walking along the beach at the time, and reported: "There was no noise at all. It was hard to believe."

The plane sank immediately, but its right wing and tail remained above water. Raymond Bouse's body washed ashore a few hours later, but Lively's body did not appear. Divers made a thorough search of the plane and the area around it. The body could not be found.

Two years later on February 1, 1982, for some strange reason, Lively's fully clothed body was found floating 30 yards north of the Channel Islands Harbor jetty near where the plane had originally crashed! Where had the body been for two years? Why did it suddenly reappear?

The bodies of other accident victims have traveled long distances by way of Channel currents before being released to the surface. A Coast Guard boat commander said it was not unusual for the body of a person drowned in the Santa Monica area to travel several months under water and emerge to the surface in the Santa Barbara Channel.

Missing Navy Flyers

The twin engined Navy propeller driven ES-2D Tracker airplane was about halfway between Santa Cruz Island and San Nicholas Island when it developed engine trouble. It was 9:45 a.m. on May 30, 1980. The four man crew was on a range surveillance and clearance mission out of Point Mugu Naval Base. The plane was flying about 100 ft. above the water at the time. The crew may have been flying over a boat warning it to clear the area for military reasons. Having both engines develop trouble at the same time is unusual. Being at such a low altitude, the pilot had little opportunity to get out of trouble. Apparently, nothing could be done to maintain power and the plane crashed in the sea about 20 miles north of San Nicholas Island.

Having signaled for help, rescue planes and boats sped to the area searching for the plane and men. In the crash the co-pilot, LT William Walters, and radarman, Petty Officer 1st Class John Tilghman, managed to escape from the ditching. A few hours later, the men were found floating in a life raft. Walters' left leg was fractured in the crash. Searchers could find no trace of the pilot, CDR Ronald G. Haugen or radarman Petty Officer 1st Class Juan De La Garza, or wreckage of the plane. Navy and Coast Guard planes and ships continued searching the sea for several days for the missing fliers, but never found them.

Some speculated that the crash may have been witnessed from a boat being warned to move. The Navy would issue no statements on the accident, however. Could the plane have been shot down by smugglers retaliating for being spotted transferring drugs at sea?

Other Channel Victims

The Channel has claimed many unfortunate flyers. On August 5, 1973, a single engine plane crashed into the sea only ten feet in front of a 23 ft. boat in dense fog at 9:30 in the morning. Divers found the 25 year old pilot's body half out of the aircraft in 53 ft. of water off the Ventura County coast. Another plane, flying low over the water banked, lost some altitude and hit a wave with his wing. The plane crashed into the sea ending upside down off Ventura's Pierpont Beach. Miraculously, the two flyers escaped with only minor injuries. Several other planes have made forced landings on the beaches.

Amphibious Plane Crashes

Planes and helicopters continued to drop into the Channel during the 1980s. On April 12, 1987, an amphibious plane crashed and burned in the Channel about 3 miles off the coast of the Rincon Parkway. The plane sank about ten minutes after hitting the water. The three Santa Barbara men aboard escaped death, but two were injured. The pilot, John Schwamm, suffered burns over about 60 percent of his body and Douglas Harlow, 22, suffered second-degree burns to his face and hands. The two injured were treated and later transferred to The Sherman Oaks Burn Center. The third man aboard, Ken Keiding, 27, was unhurt.

The twin engine Grumman Widgeon was flying low to enable the passengers to photograph sailboats, when the engine lost power and set down in the water. Apparently, the fire started when fuel leaked out and ignited during the crash. The crew of the 27-foot sailboat, *Hazardous Waste*, rescued the three from the sea.

Cherokee Goes Down

Two months later another plane with three aboard crashed about 300 yards offshore from Goleta. A Piper Cherokee single engine plane lost power at 9:30 p.m. and notified the Santa Barbara Municipal Airport tower when about 12 miles away. The plane came down off Haskell Beach. The three persons, from Riverside, California, were saved by an oil platform work boat in the area and taken to the Goleta Valley Hospital for treatment of exposure.

Restaurateur Killed In Helicopter

A strange accident occurred on September 4, 1983, when Jaime Font, 42, was returning alone in his helicopter from Goleta to Ventura after the closing of his Goleta restaurant. For no known reason, Font's helicopter crashed into the ocean off Hobson Beach on the Rincon about 3 p.m. Sunday morning.

Ventura County Sheriff's divers recovered his body from the wreckage in 50-feet of water. He apparently died from massive injuries from the crash. Font was an experience helicopter pilot who served in Vietnam. Font was involved in several legal squabbles with the Ventura Port district before his death.

World War II Bomb

Strange items are often found in the Channel, giving clues to its many users. In the late 1960s, a World War II plane was found in the Channel. Authorities had no record of the plane missing or lost in the area. On February 1, 1983, the fishing boat, *Karen, Marie* hauled in a 500-pound bomb from the floor of the Channel at Chinese Cove, on the northeast side of Santa Cruz Island. Identified by a U.S. Navy explosives team as a World War II aerial bomb, the unusual catch was pulled aboard in the trawler's net. The demolition experts boarded the fishing boat and took the bomb to the Seabee base at Port Hueneme, where they followed standard precautions to defuse the 40 year-old bomb. Experts estimate that countless bombs of all sizes are strewn across the Channel, along with many aircraft--all casualties of military operations in the Basin during World War II. Although old and underwater a long time, these bombs can still be live and dangerous.

From Sea Fever

*I must go down to the sea again, to the lonely sea and
    the sky,
And all I ask is a tall ship and a star to steer her by,
And the wheel's kick and the wind's song and the
    white sail's shaking,
And a gray mist on the sea's face, and a
    gray dawn breaking.
I must go down to the sea again, for the call of the
    running tide
Is a wild call and a clear call that may not be denied;
And all I ask is a windy day with the white clouds
    flying,
And the flung spray and the blown spume, and the
    sea-gulls crying.*

By John Masefield

THIRTEEN

STORMS, SHIPWRECKS, & DIVING ACCIDENTS -- 1980s

STORMS

Coastal Storm of January 1983

A sea level rise of a few inches in the Santa Barbara Channel, when combined with high tides and a big Pacific storm, could have a devastating impact on Channel operations and beachfront properties. Just such a storm did hit the Channel. During the last week of January and first week of February in 1983, a Gulf of Alaska storm swept into the Basin with high southeast winds and torrential rains. The storm hit at full moon, when the moon was at its closest to earth and the tides were at their highest in many years. Waves as high as 14 feet crashed and pounded the coast.

It was one of the worst storms to strike Ventura and Santa Barbara Counties in a century—the public thought. A shift in prevailing wind currents directed the winter storms of the Pacific into Southern California, instead of adhering to their normal destination over Northern California, Oregon, and Washington, and resulted in up to four times the average rainfall for the season. The storms lined up one behind the other on the satellite maps like troops marching across the Pacific.

The relentless surf, swollen creeks, and swirling winds caused over eight million dollars in damage in Santa Barbara County, and twelve million in Ventura County, resulting in a declaration by President Reagan of a state of emergency in the region.

Surf described by many oldtime residents as the worst in more than 40 years struck the Channel coast with waves crashing through houses, and smashing their way across property and onto the streets. The terrifying surf moved huge boulders 20 feet away from their places in coastal sea walls. The awesome power of nature broke up the Miramar Hotel boardwalk and scattered its parts into the pounding waves. At the west end of the Channel, sea power pushed 37-ton protective tribars at Diablo Canyon nuclear facilities aside and rendered them ineffective in breaking the power of the surging sea.

In Santa Barbara County, government facilities, school properties and utility equipment damage was well over three million dollars. More than four million dollars in losses occurred to about 100 private homes along the beachfront, including complete destruction of several houses at Miramar Beach and near Carpinteria.

On January 22, Laura Nold, 19, was swept from her automobile as she attempted to cross Refugio Creek below President Reagan's mountain-top ranch. Her body was never recovered.

San Miguel and Santa Barbara Islands were closed to visitors because of storm damage. The only access trail onto San Miguel Island from the beach at Cuyler's Harbor was made impassable by the heavy rains. Santa Barbara Island was hit by a 30-foot wave that destroyed the landing dock and stairway onto the island. Until it was repaired, landings were made only from a skiff onto the cove's slippery rocks between tidal surges.

Along the Rincon area, the pounding surf destroyed seven homes, severely damaged 37, and did minor damage to another 58. Most of the damage was to the Faria and Solimar coastal communities. At Oxnard Shores, two houses collapsed in rubble, 36 suffered major damage, and 49 minor damage. Two coast parks suffered $67,000 in damages and the old Pacific Coast Highway $640,000 in damages. Over 300 people had to evacuate their homes.

The Ventura County Fairgrounds were completely flooded and the Ventura Pier lost several pilings and some supporting structures. Holiday-like crowds swarmed along beaches to witness

Waves assault the 'Rincon' in 1983.

the huge waves and the coastal damage. Many roads and bridges were washed out and numerous mud slides started. Long-time coastal residents in their 70's could not remember a worse storm.

Storms of February/March, 1983

Al Jolson's saying, "You ain't seen nothing yet," applied to the Channel's storms. Shoreline residents had a respite of only a few weeks before being bombarded with an unbelievably fierce series of storms during the last week of February and first week of March, 1983. It did not seem possible, but the winds, amount of rainfall and waves were worse than the previous January/February storms. The storm series dropped 200 percent more rain than was normal in the Channel. Damage in Ventura to public property, flood control channels, roads, and bridges ran over 20 million dollars. Over 30 roads were closed due to the storms. Damage to crops, farm land and equipment amounted to another 15 million dollars.

Coast dwellers, buildings, and beaches previously hit by huge waves, took a terrific beating for over a week. Several thousand acres of rich agriculture land in the Oxnard Plain near Point Mugu were inundated. Some ranches were covered with water 15 feet deep. The Pacific Green Sod ranch was covered with 50,000 to 100,000 cubic yards of brown mud. The Calleguas Levee broke, spilling the raging flood water into the Oxnard Plain, the third time in five years. Two miles of the Las Posas Road in the Plain was covered with deep sand and silt. The Governor and President Reagan declared the Basin a disaster area.

The Mobil Oil Company pier along the Rincon was divided into several sections after about 400 feet of the wooden structure was destroyed. The Ventura Pier was closed, but survived the sea's onslaught with minor damage. Sewer lines broke in several locations of the county, pouring thousands of gallons of raw sewage down streams and into the Channel. The beach in front of the Holiday Inn in Ventura, normally about 100 yards in depth, disappeared. Only rocks, dead trees, logs and debris were jammed against the concrete promenade. Waves lapped against the walk's sea wall. Miles of beaches were covered with brownish brush and debris. More buildings and structures along the coast were damaged. A huge 180-foot barge anchored in Pierpont Bay broke loose from its mooring and threatened the Ventura Pier. Luckily, it missed, but it did slam onto the beach a short distance south of the pier. Long-time residents considered the storms worse than any storms seen in the Basin in their lifetime.

Breakers reached 15 to 20 feet high off local beaches. An oil rig in 60 feet of water off Point Conception was hit by 45-foot seas. Platform Hondo was struck by an unexpectedly large wave that washed three men from their perch on the lower deck of the towering platform.

Waves as high as a two-story building washed over the harbormaster's building at Santa Barbara Harbor forcing the office to move temporarily to the City Hall. The office and the Santa Barbara Yacht Club were both seriously undermined by the sea, and cars in harbor area parking lots were tipped over by the force of the waves. A serious gas leak and numerous electrical fires added to the terror of the stormy night. Heavy concrete freeway dividers were placed to seaward of the yacht club to deflect waves in the next high tide. But a huge surges of boiling water washed them away within minutes.

Morning found the Santa Barbara Harbor strewn with rocks, boards, driftwood, mud, and debris. Parts of battered boats littered the kelp-choked beaches, and slabs of concrete and chunks of asphalt were everywhere—all that remained of some of the parking lots. In a corner of the boatyard, a jumble of dry-docked vessels were lodged against the twisted remains of a chain link fence.

South coast beaches from Carpinteria to Refugio were hard hit by the pounding waves. Four houses were totally destroyed, five suffered severe damage, and 18 others were reported to have been damaged to some extent. The Goleta Pier was damaged by a loose bait barge and the bluffs at Isla Vista were eroded.

All this took place as Santa Barbara was beginning to relax after weeks of previous storms had torn the coastline into ragged pieces. March 1, 1983, is a date that will long be remembered by Barbarenos, and one that will probably never be forgotten by Britain's Queen Elizabeth and Prince Phillip.

Here Comes The Queen

Unfortunately, Britain's monarch, Queen Elizabeth II, arrived at the height of the punishing February/March storms. Normally a sunny, beautiful setting, Santa Barbarans could only apologize to the Queen for the dreadful, grey, stormy weather.

The day-long visit, planned over a several-month period by county and city officials, included the arrival of the royal yacht, *HMS Brittania,* in the morning to be greeted by a 21-gun salute from the harbor. President and Mrs. Ronald Reagan and a national honor guard along with the Air Force Band were to greet the royal couple as they came ashore in the Queen's barge. Elaborate security plans included Secret Service sharpshooters on rooftops, frogmen to sweep the harbor, bomb-sniffing dogs, metal detectors, x-ray machines, and over 250 state and local law enforcement officers, all to protect the royal visitors during their six-hour stay in Santa Barbara.

Plans were scuttled when the Channel became so wild and turbulent that it became impassable for the ocean going royal yacht. With the cancellation of plans to anchor the *Brittania* off the Santa Barbara Harbor, the Queen and her party flew over the Channel and were greeted by President and Mrs. Reagan inside an airport hanger. After an official visit to the Santa Barbara County Courthouse, lunch at the President's mountain-top ranch, and a visit to the Santa Barbara Mission, the royal couple and Mrs. Reagan flew back to their yacht in Long Beach. Continued bad weather forced the cancellation of a trip by sea to San Francisco and the party flew to the City by the Golden Gate the next day. Later, when the Channel calmed down, *HMS Brittania,* without the Queen on board, retraced the route taken by Sir Francis Drake some 403 years before when he claimed this land for the first Queen Elizabeth.

Storm of January, 1988

Starting on January 17, 1988, high winds, high tides and high waves hit the Santa Barbara Channel area and Southern California. When the winter storm, with high winds occurred at the same time as the Channel had seven foot tides, waves between 6 and 20-feet pounded the coastline. One Pierpont Bay resident in Ventura, Ron Wilson, said "They're the biggest I've seen, and I've lived here since 1968." Water damage occurred to homes, retaining walls and some public facilities along the Channel coast. Some coastal streets were flooded and beach sand eroded. Damage was worse further south in the Malibu to Redondo Beach areas.

May 1988 Storm

In a storm on the weekend of May 29, 1988, winds gusted to 60 mph and boaters were in trouble again. Two Coast Guard vessels were kept busy helping boaters in trouble which included the rescue of three people at Santa Cruz Island—two from a capsized boat.

Unfortunately, Ventura was holding its annual Fiesta del Sol on Sunday when the gale force winds attacked the party. Made of tough stuff, the 25,000 Venturans and guests weathered the 40 knot winds at the harbor. Some walked about with plastic bags over their head to keep the blowing sand out of their eyes.

SHIPWRECKS

Australian Tragedy

On March 24, 1985, three families of visiting Australians and their American hosts were returning from a visit to Anacapa Island when their 26 ft. cabin cruiser developed engine trouble. The craft began drifting toward a beach about 300 yards off Oxnard's Mandalay Beach. By the time the boat was 200 yards from shore, it was struck by a wave that overturned the boat and threw nine of the 12 people aboard into the churning water.

Adam Hellenbrand, a carpenter from Ventura, saw the accident from the beach. He and Dean Palmaro, jumped into the water and swam through the heavy surf to reach the people struggling in the water. They managed to save three, before a Harbor Patrol boat launched a search for survivors and two Navy and one county helicopter scoured the area from the air. The rescue operation involved seven agencies.

While survivors were being pulled ashore, someone reported there were three people trapped under the boat. Deputy Sheriff Mario Munoz attempted to reach the overturned craft, but strong riptides forced him to turn back. Munoz said later: "The conditions were pretty bad. It was just an incredible scene—one of helplessness. The ocean was just incredible."

When the capsized boat came closer, lines were attached and it was dragged closer to the beach. Firefighters arrived on the scene and raised the boat high enough to look into the crushed cabin. At first, all they could see was a dangling arm. They tunneled into the sand under the boat and managed to extricate the three persons trapped in an air pocket inside. Two of them were taken to the hospital and the third, Daryl Cosh, 12 years-old, was pronounced dead despite emergency treatment.

Some witnesses to the accident claimed that the authorities mishandled the rescue and that they could have taken action sooner to save the Australian boy. Others thought the rescuers had done everything possible under the circumstances.

Kelley Anne Rescue

As indicated previously, the Ventura Harbor Patrol makes numerous rescues every year near its entrance. One of the strangest occurred about 1:36 a.m. on September 14, 1985. Skip Riley, Deputy Harbormaster said that the harbor patrol crew on duty heard a Mayday to the Coast Guard. The boat's operator reported that the vessel was taking on water and was about a mile off Port Hueneme's entrance (about eight miles south).

Riley said: "We'd observed the *Kelly Anne* in (Ventura) Harbor previously and thought it might be closer to us than the operator believed." Assuming the boat operator might be confused, the patrolmen headed their patrol boat out the harbor entrance where they saw a red distress flare go up a quarter of a mile away.

The patrolmen reached the boat, *Kelley Anne*, by 1:52 a.m., in time to rescue Paul Stafford and Ed Ballard after they had boarded an inflatable dinghy. Both men were from Nevada. Despite efforts to save the craft it sank in about 40 ft. of water.

By 5 a.m., the boat had washed ashore and was destroyed by the surf. Debris from the wreckage of the 40 ft. vessel was soon scattered along the beach. The vessel had been valued at $150,000.

Chapter Thirteen

Island Chief swamped near Ventura Harbor,
March 9, 1984. (photo by Bob Wake)

Island Chief Rises to Sail Again

On March 9, 1984, two fishermen apparently ignored a small-craft warning at the Ventura Harbor and were in trouble before they left the harbor. The 40 ft. *Island Chief* was swamped by 14 ft. waves and the two men on board were soon fighting for their lives. Three teenage surfers watching the struggle paddled out and helped bring the men safely back to shore. The three boys were Alex Chianese, Clem Michel, and Brandon Passno of Ventura.

The *Island Chief*, a former rescue vessel, was banged around for several days in the surf before being hauled out and repaired. Later it was returned to the sea and became active as a fishing boat.

Sea Urchin Fishermen Encounter Unforgiving Channel Seas

A terrible ordeal began on Tuesday evening, December 15, 1987, when the *Explorador,* a 42-foot sea urchin fishing boat with several thousand pounds of urchins onboard began taking on water near Santa Barbara Island during gale winds. When the boat's captain, the owner, and crew realized that the boat was going to sink, they sent a distress signal that indicated they were having trouble in 55-knot winds and swells up to 15 feet. They reported that their position was between Santa Barbara Island and San Nicolas Island.

Six of the crew put on wetsuits and three put on partial wetsuits. They opened a bag of surfboards and jumped in the ocean as the vessel sank about 9 p.m. The crew then tied seven swordfish clusters together which acted as a buoy and helped them ride out the 17 to 25-foot high waves and high winds.

One of the men, 22-year old Jeff Pelton of Torrance, decided to paddle his surfboard to Santa Barbara Island several miles away and just visible. Jeff said, "After watching our friends get weaker and go down—Kelly hung on as best she could—I said, 'I'm going to that island.'"

The three wearing partial wetsuits did not survive the 59-degree waters and high waves and died while huddled together. The captain, Patrick Paul McQuistion of Hermosa Beach, Kelly Ann Pace, fiancee of diver Bernie Sauls, and one other were lost.

The Navy and Coast Guard sent out a helicopter, airplane and two ships and searched for them until 3:30 a.m. Wednesday, December 16th. The search was initiated again at 7 a.m., the next morning. More than 2,000 square miles of ocean was searched. Fortunately for the survivors, the 80,000-ton aircraft carrier, *USS Carl Vinson,* was on maneuvers near Point Mugu and sent a rescue team to look for them.

After 17 hours in the water, the five men were spotted among the debris at 2 p.m. by a helicopter from Anti-Submarine Squadron FOUR. Navy rescue swimmers, buffeted by the gale-force winds and high waves were lowered on cables and lifted the five to safety by slings.

When told that Pelton had gone to Santa Barbara Island on his surfboard, the area near the island was searched.

Lt. Cmdr. Steve Cox said, "We had searched the area three or four times and we were just about at the end of the search when we saw him waving from his surfboard. That was the best part of this venture. We got a big charge on the helicopter and we let out quite a yell on the radio, too."

The surfer was found about two hours after the others were found. One of the rescue swimmers, Petty Officer Joseph Oglesby, who injured his chest and face rescuing Pelton said they had quite a laugh when Pelton, a diver since boyhood, looked up at his rescuer and asked whether his surfboard could be saved, too.

Storm warnings had been sent out, and most fishermen returned to port on Tuesday, December 15th. Darrel Wilson, a veteran fisherman, who returned safely on Tuesday afternoon said, "Everybody was trying to come home in front of the storm. Apparently they (*Explorador*) didn't get far enough ahead of it." Aware of how the weather in the Channel area can change suddenly, Wilson also said that the ocean "was flat calm until four in the afternoon."

Collision of Ore Freighter and Car-Carrying Ship

One of the most serious accidents in the Channel in the 1980s occurred on September 21, 1987 when two giants collided. A 494-foot, car-carrying freighter, *Atlantic Wing*, with a load of 3,451 Honda cars, was on route through the Santa Barbara Channel in dense fog when it rammed into the side of the *Pac Baroness,* a

564-foot ore carrying freighter. The accident took place about 15 miles southwest of Pt. Conception. The *Atlantic Wing* was on route to Long Beach from Japan and the *Pac Baroness* was bound for Japan from Long Beach.

The bow of the *Atlantic Wing* slashed the hull of the *Pac Baroness* below the waterline. The damaged ship took in water immediately. The *Atlantic Wing* also sustained a nasty gash, about 50 feet long, in her bow, but fortunately it was above the water line. *The Pac Baroness* began to list to such an extent that her crew of 25 transferred to the *Atlantic Wing*. No one on either ship was injured.

In an attempt to save the ship, a Coast Guard airman was lowered from a helicopter to the deck of the *Pac Baroness*. He sealed the hatches above the waterline to create an air pocket below decks and help keep the ship afloat. Later a ship's officer and two engineers volunteered to re-board the ship and tried to restart the *Pac Baroness'* bilge pumps. An ocean going tug then arrived to tow the helpless ship out of the busy shipping lanes.

At first the Coast Guard personnel were optimistic that the *Pac Baroness* could be saved and towed to a repair facility. But later in the afternoon the ship's stern continued to settle under water. When the hull reached a dangerously low level, the three men aboard were lifted back to the *Atlantic Wing*.

At 4:50 p.m. the *Pac Baroness* slipped below the surface and sank to the bottom, 3,000 feet down. Eleven hours had elapsed since the collision. The *Atlantic Wing* continued on her original course to Long Beach to deliver her cargo of Hondas and to be repaired. The 25 crew members were transferred to another ship and taken to Port Hueneme.

Unfortunately, the *Pac Baroness* was loaded with potentially dangerous pollutants which included 23,000 tons of powdered copper, iron and sulfur concentrates—and 386,000 gallons of bunker fuel. Environmental groups were alarmed at the possible impact of the chemical on fish and other marine life in the vicinity. Shortly after the vessel sank, a three-mile-by-10-mile fuel oil slick evolved and moved toward the Channel Islands Marine Sanctuary threatening marine life. A spokesman for the company, Clean Seas Corp. of Carpinteria, hired to clean up the spill, reported that the slick was too big to contain or remove and could be dispersed only with chemicals.

Spokesman for the Pacific Coast Federation of Fishermen's Assns., the federal Environmental Protection Agency, the Coast Guard, U.S. Fish and Wildlife Service, National Oceanic and Atmospheric Adminstration, Joint Oil/Fisheries Committee and others expressed concern about how to clean up the slick and prevent harm to the Channel's wildlife. As the slick headed out to the open sea, it wasn't determined if any wildlife was impacted.

Rescues - *Celebration* Goes on Rocks

Hundreds of people continued to be rescued from the Channel due to seamanship errors, bad weather or mechanical problems. Five Santa Barbarans were rescued from the sea after their sailboat washed up on the rocks of Anacapa Island on July 28, 1989. Fortunately, the three men and two children escaped with minor injuries after they were forced to abandon their 41-foot boat. It had lost power and drifted into the rocks near East Fish Camp on the south-eastern side of the island.

A mayday call was received from the *Celebration* at 3:53 p.m. by the Channel Islands Coast Guard. The Channel Islands National Park Service responded and sent a boat to the accident scene and lifted three people from the water. They had been in the water about 25 minutes. The other two made it to shore, but could not be reached by boat due to the rocky shoreline and rough seas.

After a call to the Coast Guard a helicopter was sent from the Los Angeles Air Station to aid in the rescue. The crew of the helicopter dropped a raft which was used to reach the two on shore. The *Celebration*, from Ventura Harbor, was left temporarily at the island until the amount and seriousness of the damage could be determined.

DIVING ACCIDENTS

Mysterious Diver Death

In a tragic diving accident in August of 1985, an experienced diver drowned near Hungryman's Gulch on the east end of Santa Cruz Island even though he had air left in his air tanks. Andy Gordon, 28, went for a 30-minute dive alone. When he failed to return, the authorities called initiated a search. The next day divers found him. His death was rather mysterious as his reserve tanks contained sufficient air to permit him to reach the surface.

A Santa Barbara County Sheriff's Deputy, Tom Nelson, said that there were no signs that Gordon made any frantic attempts to swim to the surface, such as tearing off his equipment or weight belt. Everything was in place when he was found.

Young Diver Dies

One of the youngest divers to lose his life occurred off Santa Cruz Island on July 12, 1989. The Coast Guard reported that Robert McLaughlin, 15, of Malibu, and his diving partner, Sara Graves, 18, were diving in 60 feet of water in Fry's Harbor when he became tangled in lobster lines and ran out of air. He was trying to free lobsters from a trap. Graves kept McLaughlin alive for awhile by sharing her own low oxygen supply. She stayed with him until her air supply was exhausted and then made an emergency ascent to the surface to get help from the diving boat, *The Vision*. Bill Brigham dived into the water, freed McLaughlin and brought him to the surface. But it was too late.

When the Coast Guard reached the scene, the diver's pulse, heartbeat and other vital signs were undetectable. A Navy helicopter flew the divers to the Los Robles Regional Medical Center in Thousand Oaks where McLaughlin died. Graves, who showed some signs of the bends, was treated and released.

Divers Arrested

The headlines in the October 7, 1987 issue of the Star-Free Press in Ventura stated, "**Rangers Arrest 25 Divers for Plundering Shipwreck.**" A boatload of scuba divers, members of a statewide diving group, the Association of California Recreational Divers, had chartered *The Vision* out of Santa Barbara Harbor for a three day diving trip. The divers were arrested on October 4th when their boat returned to Santa Barbara Harbor after diving off the islands. The craft was boarded by National Park Service rangers, two Santa Barbara County sheriff's deputies and agents of the National Oceanic and Atmospheric Administration.

The divers were charged with taking artifacts from a state ecological reserve—a criminal offense—and illegally scavenging a shipwreck in federally protected waters (violating the National Marine Sanctuaries Act). Federal agents claimed that the divers removed hundreds of artifacts from the wreckage of the *Winfield Scott* at Anacapa Island and other wrecks, including brass hardware, bottles, copper fasterners and wood planking. The *Winfield Scott* was a steam engine sidewheeler that ran aground in December 1853.

The arrest of the divers stirred up a continuing debate between Marine archaeologists, state and federal authorities and scuba divers who explore shipwrecks and retrieve souvenirs. Authorities say wreck diving should be a look-but-don't-touch activity only. Many wreck divers disagree.

Diver Crosses Channel in Wetsuit

Three divers from Monrovia, California learned the hard way that the Channel can be very dangerous. Gustavo Pinzon, a 29-year-old chemical engineer, would have perished except for his wet suit and his courage to keep paddling after being swept off a 22-foot cruiser off Anacapa Island. On Sunday, June 2, 1985, three men, two brothers and their cousin Gustavo Pinzon motored to Anacapa, anchored their boat and made one dive before the weather became nasty. They decided to return to port. Trouble started when they couldn't raise the anchor and had to cut the line.

The trio, still in wet suits, had trouble starting the engine. Then a big wave threw Gustavo Pinzon off the boat. He tried to swim back to the boat, but couldn't make it. His cousins threw a line, but he couldn't reach it. Gustavo rapidly drifted away and out of sight of the boat.

On board the boat, Miguel Pinzon, 33, said, "There was nobody around, not even a plane. All this time fighting, fighting, trying to do something, the boat was full of water. . . .It was terrible. We thought we were going to die, too—big huge waves coming in and the boat like a little piece of paper."

At this point Gustavo said to himself, "When I saw the boat so far from me, I said 'the boat is gone, I have to do it for myself. I just tried to keep calm, to be realistic. Don't be scared, be conscious of what I had to do.'"

Gustavo zipped up the hood of his wetsuit to keep warm and started swimming, on his back, on his stomach, varying his stroke to avoid attracting sharks, and at times letting the current carry him toward the mainland. He said to himself, ". . .I'm going to enjoy the ocean.' Then I saw the sky, the moon, and I said, 'this is nice. OK, let's go again,' and started swimming."

As Gustavo neared shore, he saw lights which he learned later were generated by the rescuers of his cousin's beached boat which drifted ashore at Hollywood Beach ahead of him. On shore his cousins went for help and told authorities, including the Coast Guard, about Gustavo. A search was started.

A short distance away, Gustavo crawled ashore in the dark and banged on the door of the nearest house on Ocean Drive and said, "I need help." He got it. He had been in the cold water for about six hours and crossed the Channel from Anacapa in the dark. Gustavo was treated at a local hospital and released Monday morning.

Gustavo said there were three times that he almost gave up. The first, when the boat vanished; the second, when the sun set and he told himself, "'I can't do it. I'll die. The dark is coming and it's impossible someone can find me.'" And the third, when the current changed, moving him away from the beach. He was, indeed, a lucky person.

FOURTEEN

CONCLUSION

Storms and Accidents of the Future

More large ships—tanker, cargo and passenger—may meet the same fate as the liner *La Jenelle*, the *Pac Baroness, Atlantic Wing* and many others if the predictions for accidents and severe storms come true. Unless commercial and recreational sailors learn to cope with anticipated storms, the accident death toll will rise greatly. Meteorologist Douglas Inman, from Scripps Institute in La Jolla, says that "We are in a time of climate change." He forecasts that a new weather cycle will begin in the 1980s and 1990s that will produce more extremes all over the earth and that, as a result, seas will be rougher. Rougher oceans mean more pounding of the Basin's coastline.

Many scientists believe that we are leaving an Ice Age and that the seas will continue to rise as the ice caps melt. Some believe that the increased amounts of carbon dioxide being emitted into the atmosphere by man's activities has speeded up the melting rate of the polar caps. Such projected extremes in weather and the resultant rough seas and high surf will affect ships and harbors in the Channel. The storms of the 1980s may be a prelude of the future.

Those who make a living using the Santa Barbara Channel; fishermen, oilmen, kelpmen, divers, and crews on tankers, freighters, Navy and Coast Guard vessels and many other types of craft, periodically face great danger from its storms and unusual forces. Many of them have suffered injury and even death performing their duties. The professonals have learned to respect the brutal power of its seas.

Drunk Sailors Under Attack

Starting in 1989, MADD (Mothers Against Drunk Driving) campaigned to make boating safer in the Channel. They advocated that boaters who drink refrain from drinking and being at the helm at sea. After five people were killed by a drunken helmsman in Anaheim Bay off Seal Beach, a state law was passed that established a blood-alcohol level for intoxicated boat operators as for auto drivers. MADD encouraged sailors to designate a non-drinking helmsman at sea just as a non-drinker should drive onshore.

Unpredictable Channel

The Channel is unpredictable, but with care it can be enjoyed immensely. By gaining an understanding and appreciation of its history of storms, winds, currents, earthquakes, and other reccurring disasters that have caused marine and shore destruction, boaters can be better equipped to use and enjoy the Channel. The Channel's sea can be sailed in safety if time is taken to understand it. This applies to other sailing and boating areas as well. Knowledge of the past can provide wisdom for making better decisions in sailing and utilizing the resources of the Channel in the future.

Footnotes

1. Richard Henry Dana, Jr., *Two Years Before the Mast,* Airmont Publishing Co., Inc., 1965 (1841), p. 59.

2. Ibid., p. 59.

3. Phil C. Orr, *Pre-history of Santa Rosa Island,* Santa Barbara Museum of Natural History, 1968.

4. Ibid.

5. Zephyrin Englehardt, *San Buenaventura, The Mission by the Sea,* Mission Santa Barbara, 1930.

6. Benjamin G. Wright, *San Francisco's Ocean Trade - Past and Future,* 1911, pp. 38-42.

7. Ibid.

8. Ibid.

9. Ibid.

10. *Santa Barbara Gazette*, 1856.

11. Ibid.

12. Ibid.

13. *Santa Barbara News-Press.*

14. Charles A. Lockwood, Hans Christian Adamson, *Tragedy at Honda*, Valley Publishers, Fresno, CA 1978.

15. Ibid., pp. 236, 237.

16. Ibid.

17. Ibid.

18. Ibid., p. 159.

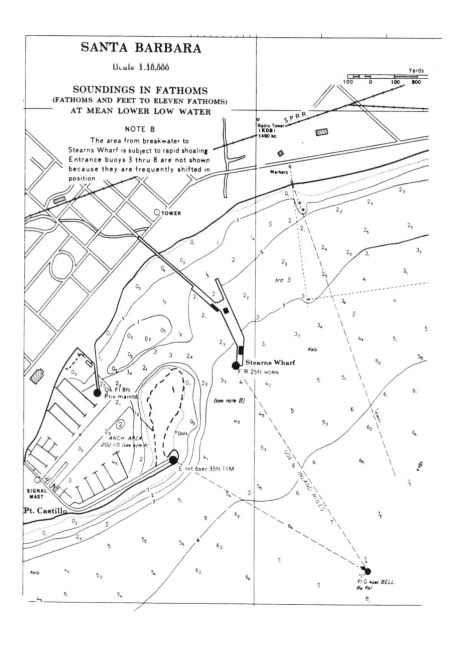

SANTA BARBARA

Scale 1:10,000

SOUNDINGS IN FATHOMS
(FATHOMS AND FEET TO ELEVEN FATHOMS)
AT MEAN LOWER LOW WATER

NOTE B
The area from breakwater to
Stearns Wharf is subject to rapid shoaling
Entrance buoys 3 thru 8 are not shown
because they are frequently shifted in
position

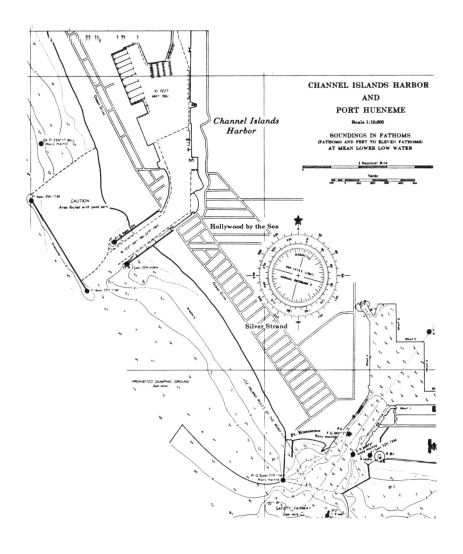

CHANNEL ISLANDS HARBOR
AND
PORT HUENEME
Scale 1:10,000

SOUNDINGS IN FATHOMS
(FATHOMS AND FEET TO ELEVEN FATHOMS)
AT MEAN LOWER LOW WATER

*Channel Islands
Harbor*

Hollywood by the Sea

Silver Strand

Pt. Hueneme

167

Port of Hueneme. (November 1976

ORDER FORM

TO:
Pathfinder Publishing
458 Dorothy Ave.
Ventura, CA 93003
Telephone (805) 642-9278   FAX (805) 650-3656

Please send me the following books from Pathfinder Publishing:

_____Copies of **Elite Warriors** Hard Cover, @ $22.95 $____
_____Copies of **Silent Warriors** @ $22.95 $____
_____Copies of **Surviving a Japanese P.O.W. Camp**
    @ $9.95 $____
_____Copies of **Agony & Death on a Gold Rush Steamer**
    @ $8.95 $____
_____Copies of **Shipwrecks, Smugglers & Maritime**
    Mysteries @ $9.95 $____
        Sub-Total $____

Californians: Please add 7.25% tax. $____
Shipping* $____
        Grand Total $____

I understand that I may return the book for a full refund if not satisfied.
Name:_____

Address:_____
_____ZIP:_____

Credit Card: Visa____ Master____
No._____

*SHIPPING CHARGES U.S.
Books: Enclose $3.25 for the first book and .50c for each additional
book. UPS: Truck; $4.50 for first item, .50c for each additional.

Shipwrecks